Me 109:
Willy
Messerschmitt's
peerless
fighter

Me 109: Willy Messerschmitt's peerless fighter

Martin Caidin

PHOTO CREDITS:

Photographs for this book were especially selected from the following Archives: from left to right page 2–3 Caidin; 10–11 Sudd. Verlag; 12–13 Caidin; 16 Sudd. Verlag; 18–19 Caidin; 21 Caidin; 22–23 Caidin; 30–31 Bundesarchiv; Sudd. Verlag; 39 Ullstein; 42–43 Sado Opera Mundi; 44–45 Sudd. Verlag; 46 Sudd. Verlag; 48–49 Bibliothek fur Zeitgeschichte; 50 Sudd. Verlag; 54–55 Sudd. Verlag; 56 Ullstein; 57 Sudd. Verlag; 59 US Air Force; 60–61 US Air Force; 62 Ullstein; 64–65 Sudd. Verlag; 68 Bundesarchiv; 69 Bundesarchiv; 70–71 Caidin; 72 Sado Opera Mundi; 72 Sudd. Verlag; 74–75 Associated Press; 76 Ullstein Sado Opera Mundi; 78–79 Sado Opera Mundi; 80–81 Bundesarchiv; 82–83 Bibliothek fur Zeitgeschichte; 84–85 Ullstein; 86 Sudd. Verlag; 89 Sado Opera Mundi/Sudd Verlag; 92–93 US Air Force; 95 Sudd. Verlag Bundesarchiv; 96–97 Bundesarchiv; 98–99 Bundesarchiv; 100–101 Bundesarchiv; 105 Bundesarchiv/Documentation Française; 106–107 Bundesarchiv; 108–109 Caidin; 110 Caidin; 115 Bibliothek fur Zeitgeschichte Bundesarchiv; 116–117 Bundesarchiv; 118–119 Bundesarchiv; 120–121 Bundesarchiv; 124–125 Bundesarchiv; 126–127 Bundesarchiv; 132–133 Caidin; 134 US Air Force.

ISBN 0-345-25888-6-250

Manufactured in the United States of America

First Edition: November 1968
Fourth Printing: April 1977

Editor-in-Chief: Barrie Pitt
Art Director: Peter Dunbar
Military Consultant: Sir Basil Liddell Hart
Picture Editor: Robert Hunt
Research Assistant: Yvonne Marsh
Special Drawings: John Batchelor

contents

Quarter century of greatness

Introduction by Generalleutnant Adolf Galland

I would like to extend my sincere thanks to the author and the editor for offering me the opportunity of writing the foreword to the book 'Me-109'. I consider it an honor to do this, since the book was written by an expert who did tremendous work and research on such a highly technical historical subject. I extend my hearty compliments to Martin Caidin. He did an excellent job. Only an enthusiast for this subject, a man who lives and flies the Me-109 to this day, can have written such a comprehensive history of this famous aeroplane.

As I started to write this foreword, my mind went back to the days when the Me-109 virtually filled my life. I first met the aircraft in 1935 when Messerschmitt's chief test pilot landed with the prototype No V-2 at our fighter base at Jüterbog, south of Berlin. He was on the first ferrying trip from the Messerschmitt factory to the Luftwaffen-Test Center at Rechlin and it was easy to understand his proud desire to show off this aeroplane.

I was a Lieutenant at the time and a fighter pilot, and I was in a position to arrange with him to carry out a dog-fight between our Heinkel 51 biplane and this fabulous but still highly secret Me-109 monoplane. Needless to say, it was easy for us to outturn the highly wingloaded Me-109, but its pilot, though a brilliant test pilot, was without any air combat training or experience. Consequently, he did not make the right use of his superiority in acceleration, speed and climb. Later on, this combat spectacle caused even more trouble for the chief test pilot when he performed a perfect belly landing with the prototype, having completely forgotten his retracted landing gear! How many of us could say that we have never forgotten?

I remember exactly how, sitting in a fighter with a covered cockpit for the first time, I checked the visibility – very critically. The chief test pilot told me that we would not need any more visibility rearwards, because nobody could attack from the rear on account of our superior speed. I was not in agreement with this statement. World War I fighter pilots were extremely critical of a fighter aircraft which had a cockpit with the visibility restricted by a covering canopy. These veterans, who were indeed the formulators of the principles of air combat, thought that they should almost smell the enemy in the air as they closed behind him for the kill.

I had been checked out on the Me-109 in 1937 in Spain, and I had my last Me-109 flight in April 1968, also in Spain, during the filming of "The Battle of Britain". This is a span of 31 years. As a matter of fact, the first Me-109 flight took place in 1935, and the last Me-109, of a grand total of about 32,000 aircraft, was built in 1960. Thus Me-109s were being built during a period of more than 25 years – a remarkable testimonial.

The Me-109 was an aircraft with a distinct character which did not forgive many pilot errors. It was known to Professor Messerschmitt and his designers that the narrow undercarriage and the odd angle of the struts and wheels caused instability in take-offs and landings, especially with cross-winds. But the mounting of the undercarriage on the fuselage was an important factor in keeping down the weight, which nevertheless rose from 2,400 kg to 3,600 kg. Many of our good and faithful mechanics later appreciated the lift, when escaping from Tunis or Stalingrad, even if it wasn't a comfortable ride when our pilots carried two of them at once.

The Me-109E1s to E9s accumulated more and more bulges because of modifications to the engine and armament and out pilots and merhanics eventually called the Me-109 'Beule' which means bulge. The Me-109 Mark F was clean in aerodynamics again, but the nickname 'Beule' was never changed.

When I was Commander of Fighter Wing 26, I always had two Me-109s at my disposal, which assured me that I would never miss a sortie or fly in someone else's Me-109. On the 21st June, 1941, I lost both. When I attacked a number of 'Blenheim' bombers, for the second time, a Spitfire damaged me seriously and in less than one minute my engine cut out. Smoke and oil indicated that my Me-109 was close to catching fire, but I managed a belly landing and stepped out, rather faster than usual, and forgetting my cigar. That same afternoon I made many mistakes, among them taking off and attacking a Spitfire squadron without a wingman. I shot down the next to the last Spitfire whereupon the last did the same to me. This RAF fighter pilot shot exceedingly well. As I began to recover from the shock, I found that my fuel tank was on fire. In such situations the parachute is a most useful and appreciated item. However, the usual attrition rate of my aircraft was not so high. I remember that I accomplished 28 kills with the same Me-109E4/N. No wonder that I developed the kind of affection for this aircraft that is normally reserved for human beings. All these and many more memories come back in reading Martin Caidin's story.

The number of those who came in touch with the Me-109 and who had some form of relationship with it runs into millions. We, therefore, thank the author for this excellent book and wish him every success.

Prologue

They cruised high over the heartland of Germany. Eight fighters with black crosses on their wings and fuselage, with swastikas on the vertical fins. Eight Messerschmitt Me-109G fighters, descendants of an airplane which had first flown a decade before, which eight years before this spring of 1945 had first entered combat. Now the forests and mountains of Germany blurred in the haze that drifted high above the land, a haze of smoke from thousands of fires, marking the final destruction of the German war machine. The Me-109Gs flew at 32,000 ft, well above most of the air conflicts that once had spread across all Europe, that now were concentrating on ever-diminishing areas as the limits of German-held territory continued to shrink. The sky more than six miles above the Reich belonged to the Allies; almost wholly, this deep into Germany, to the Americans. The fleets of four-engined bombers at times had numbered more than two thousand heavy raiders, escorted by upwards of a thousand fighters that ran free in sweep-and-destroy tactics. Now, in April of 1945, the great aerial armadas

were no more. There was no need for them. Instead, the bombers came over in formations of fifty to several hundred well-disciplined marauders firing shotgun blasts of bombs at the remaining targets. The eight Me-109G pilots looked down. Flying in stacks from 22,000 feet to as high as 25,000 feet were several hundred Flying Fortresses, an equal number of fighters weaving through the airspace all about the raiders. The German pilots scanned the skies in every direction. They could see the Mustangs, swift and deadly, prowling for German interceptors, waiting to ward off the attackers as they came in for their swift passes at the Fortresses.

The German leader must have laughed to himself at that moment. A laugh of irony, to be sure. What could eight Messerschmitts do against that terrible phalanx of American airpower? Very little, really, in terms of stemming the attack, of protecting those on whom the bombs were to fall. The war was lost. It was not yet ended, but it had been lost for a long time. Yet the pilots in the Messerschmitts never hesitated before the furious defenses of several thousand heavy machine guns in the Fortresses and the slashing intercept of the Mustangs. They were fighter pilots, the enemy was in sight. So long as they could fly and fight they would attack.

These were the final days of the Luftwaffe. Fighter pilots were hunted in the air and found no refuge on the ground. The fighters destroyed in the cascading explosions of carpet bombing were the descendants of an airplane that in the late '30's had startled the world in fierce competitions that pitted the most advanced machines of different nations against one another. The original models of the Me-109 had fought in Spain and revolutionised the air war to which they came to test their mettle. The 109 had ruled the skies from Norway to Africa, from distant Russia to England. For eight years the famed Messerschmitt design had prevailed through successive changes and modifications, and at war's end it could still fly and fight on even terms with the best fighters produced by its opponents.

It was the greatest fighter airplane ever to take to the skies.

'It was the German Air Force which dominated world diplomacy and won for Hitler the bloodless political victories of the late thirties. It was the German Air Force which subsequently led Hitler's armies triumphant to the North Cape of Norway, the Bay of Biscay, the gates of Alexandria and the shores of the Volga . . . '

In that statement by General Carl Spaatz, former Commanding General, United States Air Forces, lies the heart of the criteria by which we may judge the Me-109 the 'greatest fighter of all time'. For 'greatness' in the design of a military aircraft means more than high performance. It comprises reliability, ceaseless improvement – above all, availability.

The German Air Force which swept Hitler's armies to the limits of their conquests did so with only one type of aircraft in service. That machine, of course, was the Me-109.

Perhaps the most knowledgeable student in the Allied camp of the Air Force is Wing Commander Asher Lee, RAF, whose work, *The German Air Force*, has long been regarded as one of the outstanding documents on

that air arm. 'Until the more heavily armed Focke-Wulf FW-190 appeared in operation in the autum of 1941,' he writes, 'the Messerschmitt Me-109 was the only single-engined fighter in the Luftwaffe . . . If one takes the overall picture from 1936 to the end of the war and considers the varying factors of performance at various heights, climb, manoeuverability, speed, reliability in dive, firepower, sturdiness, etc., the Luftwaffe may perhaps claim that its single-engined fighter aircraft was either equal to or slightly ahead of its opponents until the very end of the war.'

In a final review of fighter aircraft, he states that the Me-109 'proved itself the equivalent, if not the superior, of any Allied fighter brought against it, including the Hurricane and the Spitfire . . . If the Allies had a slight technical pull on the whole, it was certainly not till the last year of the Second World War. The big difference was of course in the quality of pilots . . . By the last year of the war many of the German single-engined fighter pilots were hardly fit to do much more than take off and land the aircraft they flew. It was the German pilot deficiencies much more than the aircraft technical deficiencies which gave the Allies such complete air domination towards the end of the war.'

Perhaps the reader will question this unqualified selection of the Me-109 design as 'the greatest fighter airplane ever built.' Certainly there will be those who will point out that the Mustang was faster, more manoeuvrable, with far greater range, and better visibility. But two pilots of equal ability, one in the Mustang and one in the Me-109, would have found their machines extraordinarily well-matched.

And it is the historian who would, somewhat wryly, point out that the Mustang was absent for the many years that the Me-109 fought on such a wide scale, and much the same argument can be made against the Focke-Wulf FW-190, a superb machine which many feel to be the really outstanding fighter design of World War II. It should be remembered, however, that the Me-109 was in combat several years before the FW-190 made its

Stablemates from Messerschmitt- the
Me-109 and the Me-110 fighters

An Me-109G-6 makes a fast low-level pass over an airfield

appearance, and also that, despite its advantage of later design and the benefits of combat experience of the Me-109 and its competitors, the FW-190's performance fell off severely above 21,000 ft. For high-altitude combat the FW-190 was clearly the inferior of the Thunderbolt and the Mustang and of contemporary British fighters, and indeed, there were missions flown where the Me-109s were required to fly top cover for the Focke-Wulfs! There were also top-scoring German aces who, when their units converted from Messerschmitts to Focke-Wulfs, refused to give up their Me-109 fighters.

In this volume – a 'character study' of the Me-109 – no attempt has been made to include every sub-variant of the Me-109 series, many of which were carried out on single aircraft or were essentially only 'paper design' pro-

posals. Engineers may produce an almost limitless number of modifications to a basic design and no list can be totally inclusive, for the simple reason that many adaptations of or modifications to a design never were recorded. As for the preference for the term *Me-109* rather than *Bf 109*, in the United States, insofar as official and combat histories are concerned, Me-109 is accepted as correct identification and so it will remain in these pages. The term Bf derives of course, from the manufacturer, *Bayerische Flugzeugwerke*, which produced the early fighter models. In 1938 BFW underwent a change in title to Messerschmitt AG, and in many cases Bf 109 soon became Me-109. (For that matter, there were many other manufacturers. Of the 1,540 Me-109 fighters delivered in 1939, the design-manufacturer, Messerschmitt AG, produced only one hundred and fifty aircraft. The others were manufactured by Ago at Oschersleben, Arado at

Warnemunde, Erla at Leipzig, and by WNF – Delitzch and Wiener-Neustadt.)

More Me-109 fighter aircraft were built than were ever produced for any other series fighter – a total greater than 33,000 airplanes in the Me-109 series. No one knows exactly how many more than 33,000 machines were produced because the records themselves are suspect, especially when one considers the many sub-contractors in Germany, the thousands of Me-109 variants that were manufactured in nations other than Germany, the many wrecked Me-109 fighters that were rebuilt and listed on production records as 'new' fighters, and the sheer mass involved in such numbers-keeping. But if the exact figure may never be confirmed, there is little doubt that the Me-109 fighter was produced in greater number than any other fighter aircraft of World War II.

Many of these fighter airplanes are still serving with different nations in Europe. To be sure they now fill the role of trainers, and even the number of such aircraft is diminishing swiftly. The time is not far off when the last operational Me-109 fighter, in whatever variant it may exist, flying with a Merlin engine or some other powerplant, will be retired. At that time the role of this machine as a fighter aircraft will finally be relegated to history.

Yet the Me-109 will be flying for a long time to come. Like the other great fighters of World War II it has its champions, men willing to spend the time, effort and money to assure that there will be several models of this machine in excellent flying condition. At those moments when the original creation of Willy Messerschmitt slips upward from the earth and tucks in its gear, and raises its nose for a soaring climb above the clouds, history will be returned from the statistical ledgers to the reality of flight.

A thoroughbred is born

'Too little and too late' . . . is a phrase which would hardly seem to apply to the Messerschmitt Me-109, fighting in Spain as early as 1937 – years before the outbreak of World War II. Yet none other than Luftwaffe Inspector-General Adolf Galland insists that such was the case.

Referring to the 1940-41 period, Galland states flatly that the 'Me-109 was at the time the best fighter plane in the world. It was not only superior to all enemy types between 1935 and 1940 but was also a pioneer and proto-type for international fighter con-struction. The Me-109 did not result from demands made by aerial warfare. On the contrary, it was a gift from the ingenious designer Messerschmitt, which was at first looked upon with great distrust and was nearly turned down altogether. It was put into mass production far too late. Had this stage been reached during the first two years of the war, it would have given the Ger-mans absolute supremacy in the air'.

This story begins well before the design of the Me-109 fighter. The clock turns back to 1933, when Willy Messer-schmitt of BFW (*Bayerische Flugzeu-gwerke*) was involved in the design of several new aircraft – and an alterca-tion with the German government. Messerschmitt in 1933 produced the design for one of his most successful machines – the four-place Me-108 *Taifun* which was to see wide service as a small transport, military trainer, aerobatic performer and private tour-ing plane (and which is still in use both in Europe and the United States). It would also become the design base – the forerunner – of the Me-109 fighter series.

During the same year that Willy Messerschmitt created his Me-108 design he was also at work for BFW on the M36, an eight-place single engine transport of 380 hp. The M36, however, was being designed not for Germany, but for a Rumanian firm, and it was this fact that brought forth official displeasure. German engineers and industrialists were striving to build a new German air-power – so why was BFW working for a foreign government rather than for Germany? The complaint was brought to Willy Messerschmitt by Major Wimmer, in charge of new aircraft and their manufacture at the Ministry's Technical Office.

Willy Messerschmitt, who had endured a long and bitter feud with General Erhard Milch, didn't hesitate. He told Wimmer that the dispute between himself and Milch, who was Secretary of State for Air, had resulted in the virtual exclusion of BFW and Messerschmitt himself from all contracts with the German government.

BFW needed production orders to survive. Without such orders from Germany the company had no choice but to turn elsewhere – or go out of business.

But Wimmer knew there were other factors involved aside from the personal antagonism between Willy Messerschmitt and Erhard Milch. Many officers of the air force felt Messerschmitt's designs to be unsafe, for Messerschmitt favored the monoplane design and he had virtually no experience in the design of high-speed combat aircraft. Yet, Germany could not afford to lose the benefits of either Willy Messerschmitt or BFW.

At this point in time most German pilots – and air force leaders – were enthusiastic supporters of biplane fighters.

The key qualities of a successful fighter, they felt, were rate of climb and manoeuverability – with emphasis on an extremely short radius of turn. Being able to turn tightly meant being able to turn inside another airplane, giving the pilot the opportunity to fire at the most advantageous moments, and the monoplane design meant a high wing loading and, consequently, a greater turning radius than that of a biplane. It also meant greater speeds in taking off and landing, which in turn meant heavier and stronger landing gear and, in a vicious circle, still more weight and higher wing-loading and, finally, even less manoeuverability.

And Willy Messerschmitt believed in the monoplane rather than the biplane.

Nevertheless, Major Wimmer wanted to see what Messerschmitt could do with a new fighter design, despite the deeply entrenched ideas of the men who preferred the biplane design. Without experience in high-speed combat designs Willy Messerschmitt could easily produce a failure – and if Major Wimmer were the one to award BFW a fighter contract and the airplane proved unsuccessful, Wimmer's head could roll even faster than a cancelled contract.

There was a way out that would satisfy all requirements and Wimmer took it. Rather than commit himself solely to BFW and Messerschmitt, Wimmer's office issued to four companies – Heinkel, Focke-Wulf, Arado and Messerschmitt – the specifications for a new monoplane fighter. Those who knew the aircraft industry best figured either Heinkel or Arado, the leading biplane fighter manufacturers, to win the keen competition and no-one gave either Messerschmitt or Focke-Wulf even an outside chance.

As part of the design specification each manufacturer was supposed to use the Junkers Jumo 210 engine of 610 hp, but only Focke-Wulf was able to do so, because so few of the engines were as yet available; the other manufacturers in the design competition turned instead to the British Rolls-Royce Kestrel V engine that produced 695 hp.

Willy Messerschmitt was fully aware that no one expected him to produce the best of the four designs that would compete, but if Messerschmitt was a brilliant designer, he was also a man of perseverance. By the summer of 1934 he had assembled his design team. For his right hand man he chose Walter Rethal as Chief of the Design Office, for what Willy Messerschmitt lacked in monoplane fighter design experience, Rethel provided. Back in 1918 he had headed the design office of the Kondor Aircraft Works and he had sixteen years of experience in such matters.

Moreover, Messerschmitt, Rethel and their engineers had one distinct advantage – the Me-109 design. A thoroughbred from its inception, its clean lines and performance promised a long and excellent life for the airplane; the design team made their decision to lean heavily on its success. The basic concept was simple. Mate the most powerful engine available to the lightest and smallest airframe that could be designed around that engine – and use every element of success from the Me-108.

It proved to be the most fruitful decision in the life of Willy Messerschmitt.

In the words of a crack test pilot Squadron-Leader John R. Hawke, the former Chief aerobatic instructor of the Royal Air Force, 'The first time you get a good look at the Me-108B, you know you've got a thoroughbred before you. It just invites flight. The stressed skin metal airframe and clean lines are those of the latest designs – not a machine that came off Willy Messerschmitt's drawing board thirty-five years ago. Not 'the' fighter, of course, but its immediate predecessor in the form of a four-seat training and touring airplane. But sufficiently like the Me-109 to have doubled for it in the movie 633 Squadron'.

'The Me-108B is the finest flying machine of its type that I have ever flown'.

The first six Me-108A models appeared in 1934, and were powered with either a Hirth HM 8U engine of 250 hp, or the Argus As 17 of 220 hp. The Me-108A models were fitted with three-bladed propellers, although different propeller-test arrangements were also flown.

In 1935 BFW received a production contract for thirty-five improved models, the Me-108B, of which the most favored engine was the Argus As 10e air-cooled in-line engine of 270 hp. Seven of the new Me-108B models were produced in 1936. The following year production was delayed during a transfer of the manufacturing line from Augsburg to a new complex at Regensburg where, in 1938, the initial full-scale production line turned out one hundred and seventy five airplanes. Between 1934 and 1942 German production came to 529 Me-108 models. From 1942 through 1944 after transfer of the production facilities from Regensburg to SNCA du Nord at Les Mureaux, another 170 machines were produced and production was to continue after the war by the French.

One production batch of Me-108B models had been delivered when it was discovered that the metal skin beneath the fuselage, where it joined the wing, was structurally deficient. It was the sort of weakness that became evident in diving steeply or reefing the airplane around in tight turns. Rudolph Hess put on a dazzling aerobatic show with the Me-108B near Berlin where, to the consternation of those onlookers who were aware of the weakness, he seemed to court death with every strenuous manoeuver. When Hess landed he discovered the metal skin at the junction of the fuselage with the wings had failed, and that he was flying in a near-crippled machine. Needless to say, Hess' remarks and influential position brought swift results – and after modification, the Me-108B became famous as a sturdy, safe and brilliant performer.

The description following of the Me-108B pertains to the N108U aircraft owned and flown by the author.

The wingspan is 34 ft 5 in, the length 28 ft 7 in, and the height 9 ft 5 in. Aileron span is 6 ft; each flap spans 7 ft 5 in; each leading-edge slat spans 8 ft 10 in. The wing area is 207 sq ft.

The Me-108B is a low-wing cantilever monoplane. The wing construction is trapezoidal, single-box-spar, with leading and trailing-edge ribs, the whole covered with smooth metal sheet. The leading-edge slats are of Handley-Page design. The fuselage is of all-metal, monocoque, stressed-skin construction. Flanged oval hoops are spaced by open-section stringers, over which the duralumin stressed-skin in vertical panels is riveted, with the join down the centerline of the underside.

The tailplane is of single-spar metal construction, and is adjustable in incidence by means of a chain-screw drive, connected to a large wheel in the left-side cabin pilot seat, and moved manually by the pilot. The incidence change is used to trim the aircraft in flight. The conventional fabric-covered elevators are aerodynamically and mass balanced, and work independently of the variable incidence tailplane. The vertical fin is of single type, metal construction; the rudder is conventional, fabric-covered, is aerodynamically and mass balanced.

Ailerons are of the slotted type, fabric-covered, rear-mounted and are mass-balanced. Trim is ground-ad-

Professor Willy Messerschmitt, who designed the long-lived Me-109

Messerschmitt's design philosophy in evolution – the Me-109's predecessor, the Me-108 Taifun, shows lines like those of the fighter

justable only. The flaps are of standard design, fabric covered and rear mounted. They are slotted and provide both excellent additional lift and/or drag as desired. They provide a movement of from fully up to 48° fully down. The flaps are mechanically operated by a chain-and-gear system, by use of a wheel on the left, forward side of the cockpit wall. Any degree of flap movement from 1° through 48° may be selected by the pilot.

Operation of the Handley-Page slats is fully automatic, and they are of the non-locking design. Each slat can operate independently of the other. The slats are mounted on the wing leading edges, along the outer portion of the wing. They extend automatically at sixty three to sixty nine miles per hour, depending upon the type of manoeuver being performed. The slats give excellent low-speed control and provide a positive warning of the aircraft approaching its stall.

The main landing gear is outward-retracting and well forward of the center of gravity. The tail wheel is non-rectractable and of the spring-loaded, non-locking, castoring type.

The engine fitted to N108U is the Renault 6Q-10B, six-cylinder, inverted air-cooled, inline design delivering 230 hp for takeoff. The Ratier 1532-3 propeller is two-bladed, metal, variable-pitch, without reduction gear. Normal fuel capacity is 52 US gallons, or forty three Imperial gallons. The engine starting system is compressed air, and the system has its own compressor for recharging while in flight.

The Me-108B seats four people comfortably. Controls are conventional – stick, and individual rudder bar, with dual controls in the right seat. The right-seat pilot, however, is restricted to the flight controls and throttle only.

The construction features of the Me-108 are of special interest, since so many of its successful elements were retained in the Me-109 fighter. But an even better appropriation of the 'base design' may be obtained from the performance of the Me-108B. Although this airplane was designed in 1933 and first flown in 1934, its performance compares favourably and in many instances is superior to that of modern private aircraft of the same

type. The author's Me-108 was equipped with a Renault 230 hp engine and Ratier propeller. By using an upgraded engine of 260 or 285 hp and a modern propeller the performance would be improved to a significant degree.

The flight tests were carried out by the author and by John R Hawke, and the former aerobatic instructor of the RAF noted that 'the Me-108B has consistently produced an extraordinary reaction from the pilots who have had the opportunity to test the machine severely. The airplane is exceptional in its structural integrity and in the excellence of its workmanship. It exceeds even the most stringent requirements of American aircraft under today's severe demands.

'Its handling characteristics – sensitivity, sureness, and swift and positive response to the controls – have consistently delighted pilots. Fighter pilots with many years' experience state that the Me-108B has fighter-like response, and they are unanimous in their statements that the airplane is a 'thoroughbred all the way.' It has no characteristics to surprise the pilot and despite its outstanding performance is a safer handling machine than most aircraft produced today.

'As a trainer the Me-108B is fully aerobatic and inspires confidence in its students. The machine has a rate of roll of 64° per second – completely around in less than 5·5 seconds. When placed deliberately in an almost-vertical bank and climb so that it will stall, it will not 'climb over the top' in the expected wing-snapping stall. Instead, the automatic slats keep imparting lift to the wings when they stall out, retaining full control even under the steep-turn, high-speed stall condition.

'The safety limitations (these were exceeded by a handsome margin in the flight tests) imposed are: 'Never Exceed' Speed – 219 mph, 'Flaps Extended' – 112 mph, 'Gear Down' – 112 mph.

'Some indications of aerobatic performance –

'At 160 mph Indicated Airspeed (about 185 mph True Airspeed) the airplane has a rate of roll to the left or the right of 64° per second. It may be brought cleanly, with crisp aileron

Cockpit layout of the Me-108. The main difference between this and the cockpit of the Me-109 is in the extra width needed for the two seats

action, through a complete roll in less than six seconds.

'At 7,000 ft, with full power, indicating 150 mph, the airplane may be banked at 75° angle. The Me-108B under these conditions will complete a 360° turn in nineteen seconds. Aileron control under all conditions remains crisp and very effective.

'At 3,200 lbs gross, under zero-wind conditions, the Me-108B takes off in 1,000 ft and clears a fifty-foot obstacle in 1,400 ft from start of ground roll. At 3,000 lbs the take-off roll is reduced to

950 ft, and a 50-foot obstacle is cleared in 1,120 ft from start of takeoff roll.

'The Me-108B is 'in trim' as regards rudder and aileron at the normal cruising indicated airspeed of 155 mph and under this condition is so well balanced it may be flown 'hands off'. The maximum speed in level flight at 5,000 ft is 190 mph after takeoff with a weight of 3,000 lbs. Stability throughout all speed regimes is outstanding. Following a ferry-weight take off of 3,500 lbs the airplane was climbed to 8,000 ft where with 2,300 rpm delivering about 78% power, it cruised at 160 mph True Airspeed, consuming fuel at fourteen gallons per hour'.

In design concept the Me-109 fighter – the most powerful engine in

The Taifun owned by the author again shows this aircraft's similarity to the Me-109. Note the large radiator, larger cockpit, and larger rudder

the lightest and smallest airframe – presented Willy Messerschmitt the problem of trying to eliminate the vices that usually attend small, powerful machines of high performance. The Me-108 gave him an excellent starting point for gentle and positive control responses under conditions where control is usually critical. Nowhere was this more evident than in the stall characteristic.

'Power-off stalls with gear and flaps up,' reports John Hawke, 'are remarkably gentle, with full control throughout. The stick must be held full back, there is full aileron control, the slats pick up the stalling wing through lateral movements, and the airplane is constantly trying to recover by itself. It must be held deliberately in the stall. The power-off stall with gear and flaps down is again in a straightforward manner. There is more warning of the approaching stall, more buffeting, and the wing drop is much less likely to occur. A great deal of power is needed to maintain height with full flaps down. Stall speed in clean configuration is sixty five to seventy mph and with gear and flaps down is fifty three to sixty mph.

The excellent control response of the Me-108 through the stall envelope was a feature that Messerschmitt wanted anxiously to retain in the

heavier Me-109 fighter. Test pilot Hawke reports that 'the most outstanding feature of the Me-108B is in its resistance to stalls in what is considered the most dangerous attitude – a stall when in a tight, power-on, high-speed turn. Under these conditions of a high-speed stall, the normal tendency of an aircraft, when the lower wing stalls out first, is for a violent reaction and an uncontrolled snap manoeuver. The Me-108B avoids this by virtue of its free-moving, independently-operating slats. As the aircraft is brought under harsh manoeuver into the stall, the slat of the low wing drops forward (outward), imparting additional lift to the wing. The aircraft may be held in the stalling position – still in the high-

power, steep-bank, tight-turn manoeuver. There is a vigorous movement of the slats and the airplane will remain in the turn never fully entering the stall.'

Once the fighter competition between Messerschmitt, Heinkel, Arado and Focke-Wulf was decided – with the Me-109 selected as the fighter airplane with which Germany would lead its planned assaults on other nations – the Me-108B was given a new role. Intended originally as a small transport and personal aircraft, it was pressed into service as a trainer, especially at the fighter-pilot schools. Its flight characteristics, control systems, and general design made it the perfect trainer for future Me-109 pilots.

Trial at Travemunde

The first model of the Messerschmitt Me-109 was ushered into a Germany determined to create the most powerful air force in the world – the best kind of breeding ground for a new fighter design. The policies and programs of the German Air Force during the mid- and late-thirties were essentially determined by three men – General Erhard Milch, Ernst Udet, and Hermann Goering. Udet more than any other man was regarded as the technical brain behind the qualitative values of the GAF and, like World War I ace Goering, Udet was also an ex-fighter pilot with a keen appreciation of superior fighter aircraft. In fact, during World War I Udet shot down more than sixty Allied planes, and ended the war flying under the command of Goering in the Richthofen Squadron.

Udet was a pilot's pilot. He made certain not to rest on his laurels as an ace, but remained in the forefront of aviation after the first world war. He was a winning competitor in air racing, a brilliant aerobatic pilot, a skilled engineer and, what endeared him most of all to designers and manufacturers, a highly capable test pilot who refused to remain glued to an armchair, and who insisted on flying new and experimental models himself. Udet's firm conclusion was that no air force could long exist without fast single-engined fighters with fixed forward armament. He was even willing to accept lighter rather than heavier armament if this would help realise his primary goals in fighters – every possible advantage in speed, rate of climb, and short turning radius.

This then, was the breeding ground for the Messerschmitt Me-109.

Throughout the summer of 1934 Messerschmitt, Rethel and their design team worked steadily on the new Me-109 fighter. Every attempt was made to incorporate in the Me-109 the design features that had made of the Me-108 such an outstanding success.

Above : two key figures in the Luftwaffe, Goering and General Milch, in the centre. *Below :* Udet in the cockpit of the Me-109. After the tests the former First World War ace was very enthusiastic about the fighter

The first airplane, the Me-109V1, carried the registration numbers D IABI, and showed clearly the ancestry from which it originated. The rear fuselage, the tail, the wings and the landing gear bore the unmistakable lines of the Me-108. The fuselage had been narrowed for the one-place cockpit and a hinged canopy that swung to the right replaced the twin clamshell doors. Forward of the cockpit the new fighter was of course distinctive in its own right because of the powerful engine that had been installed.

There were other features of the Me-108 clearly retained in the fighter version. The Me-109 featured an enclosed cockpit as had the Me-108, but of the four fighters in the new competition, only the Me-109 had this characteristic. Continued also from the Me-108 design were the leading-edge slats and the slotted flaps. The gear for the Me-109 was of the same design, but a wider tread was obtained by splaying out the gear in the full-down position; the Me-108 gear came straight down from the wing, but the fighter version was splayed. In order to save weight the Me-109 gear, like its predecessor, was hand-pumped through its cycling (this was to be changed to a power system).

Of the four competitors – Heinkel, Arado, Focke-Wulf and Messerschmitt – the last design stole all honors for appearance. The Me-109 looked like a winning thoroughbred, with the sleek and clean lines pilots expect to see in a top fighter. On the ground it rested at a high angle. This resulted in poor pilot visibility while taxiing, but Messerschmitt and his team considered this a light penalty to pay for the highest possible lift coefficient during the landing approach.

In September of 1935, Messerschmitt test pilot Knoetsch took Me-109V1 (V – Experimental) into the air for its first test flight. During the next several weeks he continued to flight-test the airplane, and the design team discovered the inevitable 'bugs' that crop up in any new design. The Me-109V1 still featured the unusually narrow landing gear that had been a trademark of the Me-108, and Knoetsch complained that the narrow gear made the fighter unusually difficult to handle on the ground. He had little good to say about the mechanical operation of the gear, recommending strongly that this be replaced at once with a power system, but there was no time in which to modify the airplane. It was already expected at the Rechlin Experimental Establishment where German Air Force engineers were waiting to make preliminary tests of the aircraft.

Rechlin proved a serious obstacle for the Me-109V1. The surface of the airfield was much rougher than the field at Augsburg and the pilot had unusual difficulty in handling the machine on the ground. The Me-109V1 was so unstable in ground handling that German authorities insisted that the track of the wheels must be widened immediately, and Messerschmitt engineers, without sufficient time to return the machine to Augsburg, modified the airplane on the spot, resulting in greatly improved stability with the new splayed gear.

Far more important to Willy Messerschmitt was the initial reaction to the Me-109V1 performance in the air. No one had expected the new Messerschmitt fighter to be in the same class with its competitors, but its flight manoeuvers and its performance were so excellent that observers were changing their minds directly on the scene. Willy Messerschmitt, the word went around quickly, had come up with the biggest surprise in German aviation, and his would be the airplane to beat at the final flight trials competition at Travemunde.

The Me-109V1 tested at Travemunde was powered with the Kestrel V engine of 695 hp. The wing-span was 32 ft 4.5 in, the length 27 ft 11 in and the height 11 ft 2 in. Empty weight was 3,310 lbs and the gross weight 4,195 lbs. No armament was fitted in this first prototype of the new fighter. It reached its maximum speed of 292 mph at an altitude of 13,000 ft, and had a service ceiling of 26,300 ft.

The Me-109V1 at Travemunde lived up to the advance billing of its test flights at Augsburg and Rechlin. Clumsy it might have been on the ground, but in the air the airplane was superb. It had apparently inherited the outstanding flight characteristics and handling qualities of the Me-108, but with the greater strength, power and speed of its fighter design. Pilot reports labeled its performance as extraordinary, and there seemed little question that this dark horse of the competition would be the winner.

Arado, with a fixed-gear design, was out of the competition almost immediately, and Focke-Wulf played its hand with a parasol wing fighter. The bracing for the wing, the open cockpit, and a clumsy landing gear that retracted into the fuselage eliminated the Focke-Wulf entrant, but Heinkel's He-112V1 was another matter. The airplane, despite an open cockpit design, was sleek in appearance and impressive in performance. Test pilots determined that the two machines, the Me-109V1 and the He-112V1, were remarkably similar in flight performance – so close that German authorities hedged on a final decision of the major production contract. Instead, Messerschmitt and Heinkel each received a contract for an additional ten aircraft for accelerated tests.

To Willy Messerschmitt the contract award to Heinkel could not have mattered less. He had been considered an outsider with no real chance of success in the Travemunde competitions, and he knew the Heinkel was plagued with production problems; he figured, rightly as it turned out, that these would become so severe that the Heinkel would never receive a major production order. Further, he believed implicitly that the Me-109 design was superior to any of its competitors, and that with more powerful engines and other refinements the performance of the Me-109 would improve greatly. Willy Messerschmitt exercised his confidence in a manner that left little question of his sincerity. The second prototype, Me 109V2, rolled out of the Messerschmitt (BFW) plant without a single modification to the design, the only change in the second aircraft being installation of the Jumo 210A engine of 610 hp (using a Schwarz wooden propeller) and provision for two machine guns (MG 17s) to be mounted in the engine cowling. Messerschmitt had made it patently clear to all those who knew fighter aviation well that the Me-109 design

was that of a thoroughbred, but the design was so revolutionary, and the step forward so advanced, that problems inevitably arose which would take time to iron out. And there were also problems with the German Air Force itself; not all fighter pilots were convinced that the monoplane was the answer to Germany's needs in the air.

These fighter pilots of the old school, Adolf Galland has explained, 'could not or simply would not see that for modern fighter aircraft the tight turn as a form of aerial combat represented the exception, and further, that it was quite possible to see, shoot, and fight from an enclosed cockpit. In addition to other erroneous concepts it was feared that the higher take-off and landing speed of the Me-109 would set insoluble aviation problems. Of course all this was proved to be false in practice. Today this sounds almost like a legend from the stone age of aviation. However all these shortcomings were most painful realities at the time.'

At the Messerschmitt plant in Augsburg, the new prototypes were being prepared for their gruelling tests. The second of the new Messerschmitt fighters, Me-109V2, took to the air in January 1936 and six months later, in June, the third airplane was undergoing flight trials. Both fighters were powered with the Junkers Jumo 210A engine of 610 horsepower, the length of the airplane was increased slightly, and the gross weight rose by almost eighty pounds. Otherwise the machines were identical to the Me-109V1 in specifications and performance. Each fighter also had provision for two MG 17 rifle-caliber machine guns in the engine cowling, and this was to be the armament for the first production series, the Me-109A. But fighter requirements were changing swiftly, and the rapid change of specifications meant that the Me-109A production fighter would never be built.

Intelligence reports reaching the Air Ministry disturbed the men who were planning Germany's new fighter force. The British were reported to be developing their new Spitfire and Hurricane fighters with a performance equalling that of the Me-109

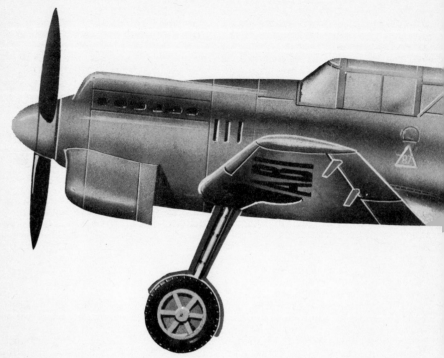

Me-109V-1
Engine: Rolls-Royce Kestrel V, 695 hp.
Armament: none. *Speed:* 292 mph
at 13,000 ft. *Ceiling:* 26,300 ft. *Weights:*
3,310 lbs empty and 4,195 lbs loaded.
Span: 32 ft 4½ ins. *Length:* 27 ft 11 ins

series, and more specifically, the British fighters were reported to have a firepower of four machine guns for each aircraft – twice the armament planned for the Me-109A. Immediately the Air Ministry Technical Office issued orders that the third airplane in the prototype series, the Me-109V3, should be fitted out with three machine guns, the two existing MG 17s retained above the engine and synchronized to fire through the propeller, while a third MG 17 weapon was to fire through the propeller spinner without synchronization. Plans were also made to replace the center gun with a 20-mm MG FF/M cannon when the heavier weapon became available in quantity. German armament experts felt that with the

heavy punch and long range of the explosive shell the Me-109 would be superior to the new British fighters armed with four machine guns.

The armament installation and tests were to take place during the exhaustive flight trials of the Me-109V series, aimed toward the first production series, which was now to be the Me-109B. Plans called for the Me-109V4, the fourth prototype, to be the first fighter equipped with the cannon.

While the armament changes and programs were developing, the airplane itself had run into its own teething problems. The flight tests carried out by Messerschmitt test pilots at Augsburg were understandably less demanding of the airplane than those tests flown by German Air Force pilots, who did their best to punish their machines under realistic combat-simulation conditions. Looking deliberately for the smallest weaknesses that operational service might magnify into serious problems,

they presented Messerschmitt with a growing list of items to be corrected or changed. The one problem above all others was the takeoff.

The Me-109 had the tendency – mostly annoying, sometimes lashing swiftly into trouble – to swing to the left during the takeoff roll. The same tendency existed in the Me-108 but was aggravated in the fighter because of the more powerful engine – and pilots had thus to be fast and skilled with their use of right rudder. When they pushed the stick forward to raise the nose they had to bring in right rudder in a co-ordinated movement, otherwise the airplane would turn sharply to the left beyond control. Takeoff with a crosswind from the left was regarded by some pilots as an unhappy adventure, and it was necessary to use right brake as well as rudder until the speed built up. Modifications to the airplane eased somewhat the left-swinging tendency but it was never completely eliminated, though in fairness to the Messer-

schmitt design it must be emphasized that skilled pilots who were aware of this condition and prepared for it had little difficulty in taking off even with a left crosswind. But the test pilots were looking ahead to that time when new pilots would be moving into the Me-109, and they felt that reducing the severity of the left-swinging tendency was vital. This was accomplished in the prototype series.

Another problem never corrected entirely was the weakness of the landing gear. Messerschmitt engineers never did build into the undercarriage the strength that many pilots felt was necessary to the machine, and in a distressing number of airplanes, including those being tested right off the production line, the landing gear collapsed necessitating major repairs. Production officials recall that once the factories were in full swing, as many as five or six brand-new fighters would be seen plowing up the runway as their gear collapsed on landing. Major fixes were made in the proto-

Undercarriage collapse, a major fault

type and early production models, but the landing gear would remain the single most serious problem of the Me-109 fighter series.

There were other areas where design and equipment modifications had to be made. In the early flights the test pilots reported severe flutter in the ailerons and sometimes in the tailplane, but was this not unusual in any new and revolutionary design. Most fighter and bomber models coming into service in any nation had to go through their teething problems: probably the best dive bomber of the Second World War was the Curtiss SB2C-4 Helldiver, famed for its sturdy and reliable structure, but in the early flight tests of this airplane (XSB2C-1) several test pilots were killed when severe vibration and flutter ripped the tails from their machines during

dives. Even the Republic P-47 Thunderbolt, the most rugged fighter ever built, killed an alarming number of pilots because of tail failures. The Me-109 was no exception to this rule, although Messerschmitt himself suffered undue criticism, his designs being 'notorious' in some quarters for weak tail structures.

The fourth airplane, Me-109V4, took to the air with many changes incorporated in its design dictated by the severe flight tests with the first three prototypes. V4 came off the factory line with its armament of three MG 17 machine guns ready for ordnance tests and as soon as the first 20-mm cannon was available, it was installed in the airplane. The first firing tests, however, made it all too clear that Messerschmitt had another problem to solve; the cannon fired with a vibration so severe that it alarmed the pilots and weakened the cannon

mounts. Pending modification of the cannon specifically for the Me-109 fighter, the next three prototypes, Me-109V5, V6 and V7, were thus built with the former armament of three MG 17 guns.

These three prototypes went through accelerated testing early in 1937 to establish the final configuration of the Me-109B-O fighters being prepared for final assembly on the production line, but even after this, long-range plans for introducing the fighter into widespread use called for the Me-109B-O series to undergo service testing.

While the B series fighters were used by operational units, advanced design work would continue with the Me-109V airplanes.

At this point the development program branched out into four distinct avenues. First, there would be the continued program with the Me-109V prototypes; second, the Me-109B and successive production series would receive service testing in the field; third, selected models would be used for competitions and demonstrations; these were to include special variants with more powerful engines to secure world flight records; and fourth, a number of the first service test models would be sent to Spain to join in combat for the acid test of battle against opposing fighters.

The Me-109V5, V6 and V7 aircraft were powered with an improved engine, the Jumo 210B. The rating for takeoff remained at 610 hp, but improved power at high altitude raised the service ceiling of these models from 26,300 ft to 29,500 ft. The maximum speed of all three models was 292 mph at 13,100 ft. (The first production batch of fighters, the Me-109B-O series, were virtually identical in all respects to the Me-109V7 test aircraft.)

Except for the Me-109V1, V2 and V3

aircraft, all Me-109V series machines were produced in 1937, although they were flown extensively for some time afterward. The Me-109V8 was the first machine to be fitted with the new Jumo 210D engine of 635 horsepower, and also the first of the experimental fighters to mount four MG 17 guns, two in the engine cowling and one in each wing. Maximum speed was 273 mph.

Me-109V8, also powered with the Jumo 210D, tested a new armament of two MG 17s in the nose, and one MG/ FF in each wing, though increased weight and a slight penalty in drag reduced the maximum speed further to only 261 mph. A modified engine, the Jumo 210G of 640 hp, installed in the Me-109V10 (no armament was fitted) raised the airplane's speed for the first time in the Me-109V series to over 300 mph; the maximum speed at 13,100 ft was 311 mph. A second Me-109V10 was built from the airframe of a standard Me-109B; this particular machine was the first to be fitted with the Daimler-Benz DB600A engine of 960 hp, intended for special high-speed tests.

Me-109V11, also fitted with the DB600A engine of 960 hp, was slightly longer than earlier Me-109V models, the new length being 28 ft 2 in. Flown without armament, Me-109V11 reached a new high speed in level flight of 366 mph, and had a higher service ceiling of 32,800 ft. Me-109V12 had the same engine, but was equipped with two machine guns and one cannon, and suffered a slight loss of maximum speed from 366 to 360 mph.

There were two Me-109V13 models. With the DB600A engine of 960 hp and a gross weight of 5,100 pounds, the aircraft had a new maximum speed of 373 mph. No performance figures are available for the Me-109V13 equipped with the DB601A engine of 1,100 hp.

Me-109V14, however, was configured to fighter category, and powered with the same DB601A engine. The V14 model weighed 4,430 pounds empty and grossed out at 5,515 pounds, with two machine guns in the nose and two wing-mounted cannon. The maximum speed at 19,700 feet was 354 mph and the service ceiling was increased to a new high of 34,500 feet. Except that the cannon armament was reduced to only one weapon, V15 was basically

identical in weight and performance.

If there was one thing the Germans appreciated as much as quality aircraft, it was the impression that those same aircraft made on neutrals and potential enemies. A nation thoroughly cowed by German military might was a nation which would more quickly come to terms in favor of Germany, and the new leaders of the Reich were determined that the Luftwaffe was to be used as a bludgeon both in negotiation and in war. Accordingly the decision was made to 'put the Me-109 fighter on show.'

Unfortunately there weren't any Me-109 *fighters* yet flying – only prototypes. Undeterred, the Germans sent the initial prototype to the 1936 Olympic Games held in Berlin where Oberst Franke put on a dazzling display with the machine, which was touted as the world's most advanced fighter plane. Meanwhile, other pilots flight testing Me-109V prototypes were still wrestling with the novel steep landing attitude, the tendency of the airplane to drop a wing just before touchdown, malfunctioning wing slots, aileron and tailplane flutter, wild swerves on takeoff and landing and, last but acutely not least, the weak attachment points to the gear which frequently resulted in collapsed landing legs.

In the year following this initial display – which for the most part had received less attention than anticipated – the world press adopted a jaundiced attitude toward this new wonder fighter being touted by the German government. Franke had made a brief appearance with the airplane, but the Air Ministry's propaganda mill had ground out such prodigious quantities of claims that the Germans were beginning to smart beneath the 'show me' remarks of the foreign press. What was so exasperating was the fact that the Me-109 was the world's outstanding fighter design – and the Germans took the next best opportunity to quiet down their critics. The decision was made to send a German team with different

Colonel-General Ernest Udet, who in 1938 became the Chief of the Technical Office in the German air ministry – a position he could not fill

Me-109 models to the International Flying Meeting to be held at Zurich, Switzerland, between the 23rd July and 1st August 1937.

German propaganda never did itself better. The Me-109's first large-scale debut produced an overwhelming reaction among the world press. The airplane, wrote the international press, could be described only as 'sensational'.

Five airplanes made up the German team – two Me-109B-1s, one Me-109B-2, a special modification of the Me-109V-10, and the Me-109V13. Ernst Udet held high hopes of winning the coveted race that involved a circuit of the Alps, and for this purpose he flew the Me-109V10, which was a basic Me-109B fighter equipped with the Daimler-Benz engine of 960 hp. During the race the still-unproven engine, fitted with a three-bladed propeller, lost power and forced Udet to crash in an open field, the impact of the forced landing tearing up the Me-109V10, and breaking the fuselage in two just aft of the cockpit. Shaken but undaunted Udet climbed out under his own power.

But there was little loss to German prestige or to their determined drive to gain international honors. Udet had to drop out, but the Me-109 design stayed in the forefront, Major Seidemann in the Me-109B-2 aircraft winning the race of 228 miles in 57 minutes 7 seconds with an average speed of 233·5 mph. And to prove the point with sledgehammer finality, the second and third place winners were the other two Me-109B fighters! The new Messerschmitts thus won a storming triumph, confirmed when Franke, in the Me-109B-2, won the Alpenflug circuit of 31.4 miles (four times around) with an average speed of 254.54 mph.

Franke then took the Me-109V13 into the single-military-airplane Alpine circuit with an average speed of 241.3 mph, and went on to win the climb-and-dive competition by reaching 9,840 feet and returning to 1,060 feet in 2 minutes 5.7 seconds. There was yet another major contest – the Alpine Circuit for a formation of

Preparing the Me-109V10 which Udet hoped to fly to victory for the Third Reich at the Zurich air races in 1937. He was defeated by a crash

The record-breaking Me-109V13, which Dr Wurster flew at 379.39 mph for a world landplane record in 1937

three aircraft. The Me-109B fighters were in the lead from the beginning, winning the event of 228 miles in 58 minutes 52.3 seconds.

At the conclusion of the Zurich competitions several sobering conclusions could be drawn by those nations against whom German military strength might one day be arrayed. In fact, the moment the performance of the new Messerschmitt fighters became clear to several competing nations, they withdrew from the air races and flight competitions, none of them doubting but that the Me-109s would sweep the field, and feeling that nothing could be gained by crushing defeats at the hands of the new German fighters.

Even then, the Me-109s present at Zurich had not put out their best performance, and aviation experts knew this only too well. The ground conditions in the Alps, the restrictions of manoeuvers to those dictated by the competitions, were only some of the factors that showed the new Me-109s operating at less than peak efficiency.

And if the Messerschmitt fighters had proven so superior to the best products of any competing nation – who would be able to stand up against an aerial armada spearheaded by these Me-109s? True, a few planes at an international meet was a far cry from an air force in large numbers, but five of the new planes had made their appearance, and there seemed no question but that the airplane was being rushed into production and would soon equip German squadrons.

Several months later these fears were heightened. The Me-109V13 had already captured the plaudits of the aviation world, and the Germans fairly ached for more of the international prestige they had reaped at Zurich; Messerschmitt therefore rushed a modified Me-109V13 for even greater honors. Into the V13 model went a new DB601 engine specially equipped to produce up to 1,650 hp for

several minutes' operation, and on 11th November 1937, Dr Hermann Wurster banked out of a turn and started the Me-109V13 down a three-kilometer speed course. He finished his run, held the airplane in a tight turn, and then sped down the course in the opposite direction. When he pulled up in a climbing turn Messerschmitt was on its way to becoming a household word in many parts of the globe. The Me-109V13 had just set a new world's speed record of 379.39 mph.

Other, more ominous developments were already under way. The worst-kept secret of the leading powers was that both Germany and Italy were already deeply committed to the Spanish Civil War, and they were to become deeply embroiled in the savage fighting sweeping Spain. To the Germans, Spain presented a golden opportunity – a ready-made laboratory for the combat testing of men, equipment, and new fighting techniques. France and Russia, too, poured supplies and equipment and skilled manpower into the fight.

The German commitment to Spain was no disguised fighting force. General Sperrle was the first commander of the Legion Kondor with more than two hundred first-line combat machines as well as fifty Junkers Ju-52 tri-motored transports in support of his air fleet. Along with the air combat units were anti-aircraft groups, communications teams, and maintenance forces.

That the Germans enjoyed a qualitative superiority in Spain could not be questioned, but that superiority did not extend itself at first to fighters. The Heinkel 51 biplanes used by the Legion Kondor to support Franco's combat forces ran into a storm of unexpectedly severe opposition from Russian-built I-15 and I-16 fighters, which clearly were superior to the best front-line fighter the German Air Force had available there.

The cry went out to Berlin – get the Me-109s into Spain!

Legion Kondor

Early in 1937 the Messerschmitt Me-109 fighter moved from promise to reality. The first small group of pre-production Me-109B-0 fighters went into service evaluation, and assignment of the B series to operational units followed quickly. This pre-production model, the Me-109B-0, was powered with the 210B engine of 610 horsepower, but as quickly as the main production line began to roll, the Luftwaffe started to receive what pilots considered the first true fighter models, the Me-109B-1 with the Jumo 210D engine of 635 horsepower. The first 109B-1 fighters went to the recently formed Richthofen Jagdgeschwader, whose pilots delighted in the performance of their new machines. At 13,100 feet the 109B-1 had a top speed of 292 mph, and from a standing start it could reach 19,685 ft in 9.8 minutes. The service ceiling was 26,575 ft. The airplane weighed 3,483 lbs empty and grossed 4,850 lbs. The armament consisted of three MG 17 guns.

From the start, however, the pilots found little to please them in their propeller, the wooden Schwarz model of fixed pitch, which restricted the performance of the Me-109B-1, especially in climb performance. Working with haste, the German government concluded an agreement to manufacture under license a two-bladed, variable-pitch metal propeller. The original designer was Hamilton-Standard of the United States, and thus the first Me-109B fighters that saw operational service on a wide scale with the Luftwaffe had the unusual distinction of being fitted with British wing slats and an American propeller.

The Me-109B-2 that would soon follow the first production aircraft was also the last of the B-series fighters. The engine was changed, first to the Jumo 210E of 640 horsepower, fitted with a two-stage supercharger which increased the service ceiling, and then to the Jumo 210G of 670 horsepower, improving slightly the overall performance of the air-

An Me-109B-2 of the type which the Legion Kondor used so successfully in Spain. The operational knowledge gained here stood Germany in good stead at the beginning of the war

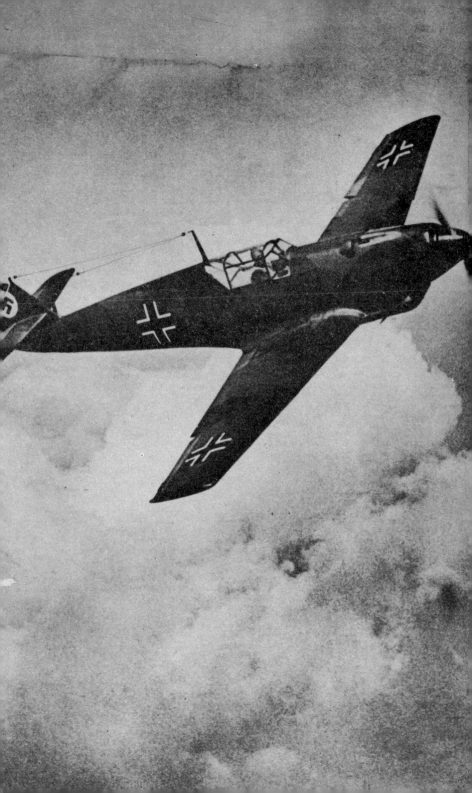

Me-109B-2
Engine: Junkers Jumo 210Ea or G, 680 or 700 hp. *Armament:* 3 x 7.9-mm machine guns. *Speed:* 279 mph at 13,100 ft. *Ceiling:* 31,200 ft. *Weight:* 4,857 lbs loaded. *Span:* 32 ft 4½ ins. *Length:* 28 ft 6½ ins

plane. During the service life of the B-series fighters, many of the early models were refitted with the more powerful engines and the variable-pitch propellers to uprate their performance.

Meanwhile, transitional training from biplane fighters to the new Me-109B fighters promised its own share of difficulties . . .

Every air force, through its leaders, must suffer certain deficiencies. The Germans, for example, failed to foresee future needs for long-range heavy bombers escorted by fighters of equal radius of action – a failure that would cost them dearly. Other nations, especially the Japanese, failed by not

anticipating the requirements of massive training programs. It was in this area that the Germans properly foresaw the future – just so long as that future clearly held victory in sight.

In 1935 Goering and his staff rapidly and totally reorganized flight training for the Luftwaffe. As a result, what had originated as a system of sport and commercial flight schools was overhauled completely, and by 1936, military flight training in Germany was on a full-scale wartime basis.

Before the aspiring German pilot had the chance to try his wings he first went through six months of gruelling infantry and basic training in order that he would 'fit' more properly the military ideal of what the disciplined flyer should be. The first six months in the Luftwaffe included more than its share of goose-stepping, firing infantry weapons, and interminable hours on the parade ground, though along with the foot soldier's requirements the Luftwaffe cadet was

taught the rudiments of radio communications and map reading. Once he had survived his introduction to military life, he either went to another school for elementary aviation indoctrination, or was shipped direct to primary flight training. Before World War II began the Luftwaffe enjoyed the riches of about fifty basic (primary) flight training schools spread throughout the Rhineland, Saxony, Silesia, Bavaria, East Prussia and Pomerania. (During the war more flight schools were set up in the areas of the occupied countries.)

Before he received his pilot wings the German cadet went through approximately one hundred hours of flight training. He moved on to specialized courses either as a bomber, reconnaissance or fighter pilot, continuing his training in light, low-powered machines, and starting cross-country flights on his own. The next course brought the student into airplanes of the Me-108B class (Gotha 145, Focke-

Wulf FW-56, Arado Ar-96). The student selected as a fighter pilot, after completing this second post-graduate schooling, would graduate to some fifty hours' training in fighters. Initial training was usually flown in obsolete biplane fighters and then in the early versions of the Me-109 series. Finally the neophyte went into the Messerschmitt Me-109 and FW-190 operational fighters, where his touch at the controls was honed to a fine degree and he was trained in operational procedures. Normally formation flights were flown at low and medium altitudes and finally to 27,000 feet. The pilot would then be permitted to fly on his own to 35,000 feet and sometimes even higher. He would be taught air-to-air gunnery, strafing, dive-bombing, dogfighting manoeuvers, bomber interception and attack, and whatever other combat manoeuvers were current at the time.

The German system was efficient and produced excellent pilots. It was quite similar in basic content to the

41

flight training of American and British pilots. It came apart at the seams as Germany moved closer and closer to defeat. The number of training hours was reduced sharply, modern military aircraft were in short supply, instructors were yanked from the schools for pressing military needs, and, finally – the inevitable result – the quality of pilots suffered. But that was later in the war, and in the late 1930's the German pilots enjoyed all the benefits of an élite training group.

As was to be expected the German fighter pilots making their transition from the Heinkel and Arado biplane fighters had more than a normal share of headaches. The agile, lightweight biplanes were an entire generation behind the Me-109B airplanes, and there was more involved than simply learning the controls and characteristics of the new monoplanes. Special emphasis was placed on training in the Me-108B which to a great extent duplicated the cockpit controls and flight characteristics of the Me-109B fighters. The single greatest problem was that the pilots, unused to retractable gear, often forgot to lower the gear before landing and slid down the runway on the belly of the airplane. In the Me-108B trainer the presence of an instructor usually avoided this sort of nonsense, but it was a common error of pilots making their solo flights in the Me-109B.

Well before most pilots had the opportunity to fly the new fighters, the Me-109B airplanes were being prepared for their initial combat debut in Spain, where the pilots of *Jagdgruppe* 88's three squadrons would pit the new fighter against the enemy. Most especially the Germans wanted to test the Me-109 against the Russian I-15 Chato and I-16 Rata fighters that were giving the Heinkel He-15s such a hard time.

The fighter component of the Kondor Legion was made up originally of four squadrons, or *staffels*. In January of 1937 they were having fair success in their actions in the Madrid area against the enemy, but starting

The introduction of fully automatic variable pitch propellers greatly improved performance. Here its operation is explained to new mechanics

Typical operational airfield scene during
the Spanish Civil War

in February, they were transferred to the Northern Front, where the German pilots found their Heinkels badly outclassed by the Russian-built fighters opposing them. Demands for the Me-109's became more insistent and the entire initial production order of Me-109B-2 fighters started on their way to Spain. By July, the first and second *staffel* of *Jagdgruppe* 88 had been re-equipped with twenty-four Me-109B-2 fighters, and the question of air superiority was soon decided. Against the Russian fighters the Me-109B proved the quality machine.

Most of the Me-109B missions consisted of bomber escort and occasionally the Messerschmitts were turned loose for low-level sweeps (the He-51s were assigned to ground attack duties after arrival of the Me-109Bs),and by the late summer of 1937 there were enough Messerschmitts on hand to increase J.88's strength with the new fighter until, finally, in April 1938 at La Cenia, the Germans prepared to turn the group into an all-Me-109 force. By now several pilots flying with J.88 were chalking up aces' scores with the Me-109s, including many of the men – Lutzow, Harder, Galland, Pitcairn – who would become the leading aces of World War II. Later, Werner Moelders would lead the third *staffel* of J.88 when in August 1938 that unit was equipped with Me-109C-1 fighters, and Moelders would continue in combat as the leading German ace of the Spanish Civil War with fourteen kills.

The Germans sent to Spain forty-five Me-109B-1 and B-2 fighters and twelve Me-109C-1 airplanes – a total commitment of fifty-seven production series fighters. (The highest strength at any one time for the Legion Kondor was forty-eight machines.) In addition to the production fighters, by the beginning of 1937 German pilots were testing under combat conditions the Me-109V4, V5 and V6 prototypes. The 109V4 firing tests with the 20-mm MG/FFM cannon were far from satisfactory owing to severe vibration, but several 109B-2 models were equipped

Galland and Moelders, great aces of The Second World War, began their careers with the Legion Kondor

with the cannon and used the weapon with success in combat. While combat tests went on, engineers at Augsburg equipped the Me-109V8 to take two MG 17 weapons in the wings, but the airplane simply wasn't ready for such an installation without major wing modifications. When the guns fired, the wing fluttered dangerously, forcing strengthening of the wing leading edges and changes in aileron design.

The 109V9 (based on the 109B-2) was then tested with a 20-mm cannon in each wing root but flutter, so bad that it threatened to destroy the wing, made it clear that the single spar of the Me-109 design must undergo major strengthening to absorb the tremendous vibration of the cannon firing. Because of the cannon difficulties, the Me-109V8 was accepted as the prototype for the Me-109C production series, and the Me-109C-0 and C-1 fighters, except for a Jumo 210G engine and the armament of two nose and two wing machine guns, were identical to the Me-109B-2 machines. As the C models went into production, engineers at Augsburg continued their armament experiments.

Group Captain J. E. Johnson of the RAF, Britain's number one ace of World War II, reviewed German fighter tactics with the Me-109s in Spain –

'Before the war our own fighter squadrons, together with those of other countries, flew in compact formations built up from tight elements of three airplanes. Such formations were ideal for spectacular flypasts, and although every fighter pilot must be able to 'formate' closely on his leader to climb through cloud, this close style was to be of little value in the great air battles.

'In Spain the German fighter pilots soon realized that the speed of their 109s made close formation impracticable for combat. The large turning circle of the curving fighters dictated that a loose pattern was the only method in which individual pilots could hold their position in the turn and keep a sharp lookout at the same time. The high closing speeds, especially from head-on position, made it essential to pick out and identify

[1] *Wing leader,* by Group Captain J E Johnson Ballantine Books

Another variant which saw service in the Spanish theatre was the C-1 with heavier armament. These aircraft are on an airfield just after the invasion of France

An Me-109C-1 being readied for a
sortie from a forward airstrip

enemy aircraft as soon as possible, so
that the leader could work his way
into a good attacking position. The
simple requirement was for a loose,
open-type of combat formation with
the various airplanes flying at separated heights which would permit
individual pilots to cover each other
and search a greater area of sky than
before.

'Credit must be given to the Germans for devising the perfect fighter
formation. It was based on what they
called the *rotte*, that is, the element
of two fighters. Some two hundred
yards separated a pair of fighters and
the main responsibility of the number
two, or wingman, was to guard his
leader from a quarter or an astern
attack. Meanwhile the leader navi-
gated his small force and covered his
wingman. The *schwarme*, four fighters,
simply consisted of two pairs, and
when we eventually copied the Luftwaffe and adopted this pattern we
called it the 'finger-four' because the
relative positions of the fighters are

similar to a plan view of one's finger-
tips'.

The Germans developed to a fine
degree their new formation tactics.
The *rotte* and the *schwarme* comprised
the most manoeuverable elements of
German formations and for patrol or
larger grouping of planes, three
schwarme made up the *staffel*. Much
credit was given to these tactics for
the German fighter success in Spain,
one writer reporting that the 'combination of new aircraft and improved
tactics brought the German fighter
pilots immediate successes. Lt. Balt-
hasar, for example, shot down four
Ratas (Another popular name for the
Mosca, or I-16) in six minutes. Captain
Schellmann increased his score to
eight and Adolf Galland reached
seven . . .'

The first 109s that arrived in Spain
were transported to Seville for assembly by some of the same crews that
had performed this task when the first
Heinkel He-51s arrived in the country.
By this time, they had learned the
advantages of speed of assembly from
their enemies, for the Republicans had
the ability to get their 1-15 fighters

out of their shipping crates and into the air within days of arrival behind the lines. The Germans now spared no efforts to reach a similar quick response with their 109s, and thereby gain an element of surprise. They did precisely that, to the credit of their ground crews.

Republican intelligence could only be described as inadequate at this time, and Republican pilots knew nothing about the Me-109 until the Battle for Brunette (July 1937) when the first Me-109s showed up in combat. They flew top cover for several squadrons of Heinkel He-111 twin-engined bombers that were attacking ground troops with formation 'carpet bombing' experiments, and the Republican pilots, who knew nothing about the 109 or its speed, were in position to 'bounce' the bombers. They weren't too concerned about the opposing fighters, for experience had taught them that they could easily outfight the He-111s, after which they would take care of the stange *monoplano* fighters higher up.

Later, one of the Republican pilots was to write – 'Our fighters went after the Heinkels but they themselves were bounced by the 109s. That ship could *dive*.' Most of the Republican pilots were also quite disconcerted by the gunfire coming out of the engine shaft. Most airmen who weren't there and were told about this simply didn't believe it. They were sure the pilots were mistaken. Not until much later was it confirmed that the new German fighters were firing through the propeller hub.

'It's most important to remember that we didn't know anything about the new fighter specifically as the Me-109. All we knew was that this was a new '*fascist monoplano*.' More than any other single factor, the surprise introduction of the 109 turned Brunette from an impressive Republican offensive into a Phyrric stalemate that the Republicans simply couldn't afford. It was a devastating loss.

'We lost one hundred and four Republican airplanes and approximately twenty-five thousand men. The Nationalists of Franco lost only twenty three aircraft and about ten thousand men. But once the initial surprise passed and we had time to look at the new Me-109 a bit more carefully, we considered it a plane to respect – but something to beat hell out of any time we encountered one'.

'The Mosca was still about ten miles per hour faster, flat out, than the Me-109. We had more power. The Mosca gave us a faster rate of climb and we had a rate of roll that was far superior to the 109. Add to that our manoeuverability; we could turn inside the 109 without trouble. All this meant, of course, that the Mosca was a better fighting machine. We also had four guns to their three and found that we carried quite a bit more ammo. We had 750 rounds per gun to the 109's 500 rounds per gun, but we didn't know this until the first 109 was captured after a forced landing.

'If I had the choice for a dogfight I'd pick the Mosca hands-down over the 109s we fought in Spain. It's true that the Mosca was pretty much at the tail end of its development and the 109 was only getting started. But in Spain the Mosca was the better fighter .

Looking at it with some perspective, the 109 certainly did prove itself in Spain and, of course, it was put into mass production. I don't want to deprecate an excellent airplane. The comparisons with the Mosca are of that time period and the new developments of the 109, into the E and F models, not too long afterwards, made it the fighter to beat.'

'But fortunately for us more than a few Germans in high places still had their reservations about the 109. Galland has made the point again and again that production was slow and proceeded in all sorts of fits and starts. At the beginning of 1940 the production was around only one hundred and twenty five a month. At the beginning of 1942 it was about twice that figure, maybe two hundred and fifty planes a month. Can you imagine what might have happened had Speer taken over production sooner? In the fall of 1944 the factories under his control were turning out 2,500 Me-109s every month!

'Maybe the trouble we gave the Germans with the Moscas we flew had something to do with it. Certainly you couldn't claim the 109 was a world-beater on the basis of plane-to-plane combat with the Mosca . . .'

Me-109R: the plane that never was

With combat experience from Spain feeding into the growing technical reserve of Messerschmitt, Germany moved steadily toward the final Me-109 design with which it could equip the Luftwaffe in large numbers. When the air war drew to a close in Spain in March of 1939 the new Me-109s had triumphed over all opposition with the exception of the Mosca fighters. Thousands of pilots and ground personnel had been blooded successfully, tactics and equipment were adapted to the lessons of war, weaknesses had been corrected and strengths exploited. Then came the heady triumph of the occupation of Austria and the Sudetenland in 1938, and the drives into Czechoslovakia and Memelland in the spring of 1939. In each of these movements the Luftwaffe displayed hundreds of fighters and bombers and transports, thundering through the skies in precise formations, lending weight to the myth of invincibility the German propaganda machine was fostering in the Luftwaffe.

Yet the boasting was far from hollow. By the time of the Munich Agreement the Luftwaffe had grown to four thousand aircraft counted in first-line machines, an explosive increase in four years from only a thousand combat-ready planes in 1935. More important, the German Air Force had been tested to some degree in battle and was far better equipped in aircraft, men, tactics, support and morale than the Czech, Polish, French and British air forces who would become its adversaries.

Through it all the key to success was the Me-109.

The 960 hp Daimler-Benz DB600 engine provided the impetus to the next round of Me-109 fighters. Engineers placed the DB600 in the airframe of a standard Me-109B to create the Me-109V10, and then installed the production model DB600A engines in the V11 and V12 models. The production series Me-109D resulted from airframe-engine experiments with the 109B and 109V series, though the final performance figures of the test models is open to question. Nowarra claims the Me-109V12 had a top speed of 360 mph and a service ceiling of 32,800 ft, but William Green, an equally well known historian in aviation matters, insists the Me-109V11 and Me-109V12 prototypes had a top speed of 323 mph and a service ceiling of 31,170 ft. The disparity of some forty mph is difficult to understand, and is complicated by further details of weights and altitudes at which maximum speeds were registered.

There is no question that the performance of the prototypes, as reflected in the Me-109D series, resulted in a fighter vastly improved over the B and C series, and the first combat plan unquestionably superior to any of the opponents against which it might be arrayed in battle. For while the RAF was driving anxiously to produce its Spitfires and Hurricanes. indeed while these airplanes were still in the testing stage, the Me-109 series was in widespread operational service.

Despite the outstanding performance of the Me-109D-0 (in production in 1937) and Me-109D-1 (in production during 1937-38), they were destined for only a brief life as front-line Luftwaffe fighters, and were produced for only a short time and in limited quantity.

Approximately 250 of the 109D-series fighters were produced before the factory ended its manufacturing run, but this brief limelight for the Me-109D-series in no way reflected any shortcomings in the machine. In fact, three had been sold to Hungary and ten to Switzerland, the Swiss immediately testing the new German fighter against the Morane-Saulnier MS-496 fighters they had purchased from France. In simulated combat the Me-109D proved superior in almost every performance respect to the French fighter.

The demise of the Me-109D was brought about by the unexpectedly quick availability of the new Daimler-Benz DB-601A engine, which eliminated the carburetor in favor of a direct fuel injection system, and also mounted a higher capacity supercharger. The end result was an engine of 1,000 horsepower which, coupled to a three-bladed propeller (used on the Me-109D was well), promised what would be unquestionably the outstanding fighter plane in the world.

To emphasize better the place in aviation history of the Me-109E, this was the first true full-production model of the Messerschmitt fighter series. It was the airplane to which, by the close of 1939, the German nation had committed itself for all-out war, and by this time it had replaced every other fighter of the Luftwaffe for operational front-line service.

Predecessor-prototype to the Me-109E fighters was the Me-109V14 which took to the air for the first time in the summer of 1938, its armament including two nose guns and two cannon in the wings. The Me-109V15 was identical to the V14 except for a weapons arrangement of two nose guns and a single 20-mm cannon firing through the propeller hub; there were no weapons in the wings. As it happened the Luftwaffe opted for the heavier armament of the V-14 model, and ten Me-109E-0 pre-production fighters were ordered, for first flights in late 1938. Despite the urgent requirements for wing cannon, the Me-109E-0 models and the first group of Me-109E-1 production fighters were fitted with machine guns (MG 17) in the wings rather than cannon, for Willy Messerschmitt was still working day and night with the WeaponsCentre at Tarnewitz in the attempt to solve the wing-mounting problems of the cannon.

The first Me-109E-1 fighters were flying in early 1939. By August of the same year, when war broke out after the German invasion of Poland, thirteen groups, each of forty fighters, were in first-line service while a total of 1,085 Me-109 fighters of all types were in active service. Eight hundred and fifty of these were of the E-series, and the remainder – the older D-1 mark – were relegated to special attack forces. By the end of 1939, production had reached a total of 1,540 Me-109E fighters.

The Me-109E-1 had a wingspan of 32 ft 4.5 in, a length of 28 ft 4 in and with the tailwheel on the ground, a height of 7 ft 5.5 in. It weighed 4,360 pounds empty and grossed out normally at 5,400 lbs, the wing area of 174 sq ft gave a wing loading of 32.1 lbs per sq ft. Equipped with two nose guns and two wing-mounted cannon it had a firing rate of 290 rounds per minute.

The maximum speed was 354 mph at a height of 12,300 ft. Immediately after takeoff the 109E-1's rate of climb was 3,600 ft per minute, the service ceiling was 36,000 ft and the absolute

Two views of the Me-109D-1. The D series had a far better performance than its predecessors, but soon gave way to the E series with its fuel-injection engine

ceiling 37,500 ft. At 62.5 per cent rated power, the most economical cruising speed, the range was 412 miles at 16,400 ft; this included fuel allowance for takeoff and climb at full throttle to the cruising altitude. The fighter-bomber variant was the Me-109E-1/B which could carry either one 550-pound or four 110-pound bombs. When diving from high altitude the pilots were instructed to descend at 403 mph while from lower heights the best diving speed was 373 mph. The maximum permissible diving speed, the redline, was 446 mph indicated airspeed.

During the period that the Me-109E and its variants were being rushed into operational service as Germany's first-line fighter, the Nazi government was in the midst of an elaborate scheme which would accomplish, simultaneously, several important

Above: The Me-109V14, prototype for the E series. *Right:* A fine study of a production model Me-109E, which was to be the Luftwaffe mainstay in the Battle of Britain in 1940

national goals. In order to prove to the world that Germany's aircraft were the best in any air force, Messerschmitt was instructed to proceed with plans to raise the world absolute speed record to a figure which most engineers thought impossible – well over 450 mph at low altitude in level flight. At the same time that this speed record was to be attained, the record-breaking airplane was to be presented to the world press not as a machine modified drastically for the record attempt, but as a standard fighter aircraft of the German Air Force.

In April of 1939 world aviation was shaken by the news that a Messerschmitt Me-109R had set a new absolute world speed record of 469.22 mph. The pilot's name was given as Fritz Wendel.

For years that record-breaking flight – ratified by the Federation Aeronautique Internationale (FAI) remained on the books as having been achieved by the Messerschmitt Me-109R and it is *still* on the record books – but the identification of the Me-109R is a sham. For the record flight had nothing to do with the Me-109 fighter, and the airplane involved was actually the Me-209V1, a wholly different design that set a world speed record which still remains unbroken to this day! Yet it was a ghastly failure as a fighter airplane and was, in the words of its test pilot, Wendel, a 'diminutive monstrosity.'

Not until well after World War II did the truth about this matter seep out and the outside world learn that the Me-109R was a fictional designation. The Germans played their propaganda hand well. As a result, a German airplane, identified as a fighter aircraft, had proved itself much faster than anything in the air, anywhere in the world, and the record had been sanctioned by the international body authorized to confirm record flights. Germany's move paid off – the leaders of many governments were convinced that Germany had an operational fighter capable of more than 450 mph in level flight.

The race for speed in terms of world records was actually a bitterly fought contest between Heinkel and Messerschmitt. On 11th November 1937 the Me-109V13 set a new world speed record of 379.38 mph, and on 5th June 1938, Ernst Udet broke the record with a 62-mile speed run of 394.6 mph. The world was informed that the airplane flown by Udet was the new Heinkel He-112U fighter; it was nothing of the sort, but the Heinkel He-100V2 prototype of the experimental He-100-series fighter.

Nine months after Udet set his speed record over the sixty two mile circuit, Heinkel played its hand for the absolute speed record in straight flight. Again the airplane was identified as the He-112U, in reality it was the He-100V8, and on 30 March 1939 it secured the world record honor for Heinkel

with a speed run of 463.945 mph.

The celebration didn't last long Several weeks later Wendel flew the Me-209V1 – alias the Me-109R – down the speed course at the new record of 469.22 mph average for the record attempt.

The speed battle – and the quest for new fighters that would one day replace the Me-109 began in 1937. Messerschmitt received authorization to proceed with a new fighter design known as the Me-209 (company project designation P.1059), and started the construction of three prototype aircraft, the Me-209V1, V2 and V3. Heinkel launched its own advanced fighter design at the same time the He-100, and although the Heinkel airplane was considered by many objective observers as the superior of the competition, Messerschmitt was so solidly entrenched in the Luftwaffe, with so many influential friends, that the Heinkel He-100 never stood a chance to make the grade.

If nothing else, the Me-209 was one of the most rakish and beautiful designs ever to take to the air. It bore little resemblance to the Me-109 series, for the fuselage was considerably shorter and the main landing gear, folding inward, was much wider than that of the Me-109. Messerschmitt placed the cockpit far back on the fuselage and designed the vertical fin to extend both above and below the fuselage and every step was taken to assure a clean design with a minimum of drag. The nose carried an oil cooling radiator, but this was the only serious protuberance, and instead of the conventional radiator surfaces for engine cooling, Messerschmitt adopted an evaporation cooling system that required 48 gallons of water. Once the heated water moved through the engine it was fed to the narrow wings where it condensed and was repumped back into the engine for further cooling. This system was almost worthless for a fighter aircraft since the water loss was about a gallon per

The Me-209V1 sets up a new world speed record of 469.22 mph on April 26, 1939. For propaganda purposes the aircraft was called an Me-109R to try to persuade the world that Germany had fighters as fast as this

minute at cruising speed and one and a half gallons at full power. At best it was a temporary solution to the serious need for cooling the powerful engine – and it gave the engineers enormous trouble throughout its lifetime.

The Me-209V1's engine produced 1,400 horsepower and that of the Me-209V2 and V3 1,100 hp for normal rating. However, the DB601A engines in these machines could be overboosted for several minutes to 1,400 hp and for a period of approximately one minute the modified DB601A would deliver 2,300 hp; but, after one maximum-power run the engine was worthless wreckage. For a speed record attempt the cooling water quantity was increased to one hundred gallons and the rate of usage went up to two gallons per minute. Carrying one hundred and ten gallons of fuel the Me-209V-series could remain in the air about thirty five minutes.

As a fighter the Me-209 was a magnificent sight – but there all resemblance to a fighter vanished. The new engine ran rough and the coolant system proved inadequate to its task. Exhaust fumes collected so heavily in the cockpit that the pilot was forced at all times to wear an oxygen mask, while in hot weather he was drenched in perspiration because of inadequate ventilation. At high speeds the fairing doors for the landing gear blew open and in emergency descents the pilots found it impossible to lower the gear at speeds exceeding 155 mph. Another high-speed problem occurred when the fuel tank caps blew away without warning – and to add to the woes of the already unhappy pilot the hydraulic system for the gear had the nasty characteristic of spraying oil over the cockpit canopy.

These were only some of the major mechanical problems. The pilot also faced a takeoff run that was long and always adventuresome because of sudden swerving tendencies – all to be mastered from a cockpit view that at best was 'very restricted'. While during steep climbs the Me-209 proved to be unstable so that the pilot was

always fighting off a tendency to stall and snap a wing down. At high speed the nose tended to pitch up, demanding constant vigilance to avoid a sudden high-speed stall during steep turns at high speed, the Me-209 lost stability and flipped wildly over on its back. Throughout all such manoeuvers the control forces were severe and quickly exhausted the pilots.

Original plans called for Wendel to fly the Me-209V1 for the attempt on the world speed record, but on 4th April 1939 the engine failed during a test flight and the airplane crashed, though Wendel escaped without serious injury. The M3-209V3 wasn't yet ready for the record attempt so Wendel was required to use the first model, the Me-209V1 – and this he did to bring home the record – flying the 209V1 twice along the course of 1·8 miles at a height of approximately 300 ft. The record-breaking plane spanned 25 ft 7 in across the wings, was 25 ft 7 in in length, and weighed 4,770 lbs fully loaded.

Once the record-breaking attempts were out of the way, Messerschmitt produced the Me-209V4 to take up the problem of developing the fighter replacement for the Me-109E series. The fuselage of the 209V4 closely resembled its predecessors, but a new wing was considerably wider, featuring the automatic leading-edge slots of the Me-109 series and after several flights Messerschmitt abandoned the surface evaporation cooling system to revert to radiators beneath the wings, which cut down speed. Armament tests included different arrangements of machine guns and 30-mm MK 108 cannon but none proved successful.

Modifications came thick and fast. The radiators were redesigned several times, the new wing slots were abandoned for drooped leading edges. But when the tests were done and evaluation was necessary it was the consensus of opinion that the Me-209V4 wasn't that much better than the production Me-109E fighters, and it was far more difficult to fly.

Yet by one of the great quirks of fate in aviation, the record set by the Me-209V1 – presented to the world as the Me-109R – of 469·22 mph still stands as the fastest piston-engine speed run at low altitude ever flown.

Willy Messerschmitt congratulates Flug Käpitan Fritz Wendel after the record breaking flight

The Luftwaffe strikes

On September 1st 1939, Hitler unleashed his armies and his air force against Poland. The Poles put into the air rather less than seven hundred aircraft to stem the German (and the Russian) onslaught, and for the most part these machines were of a performance far beneath that of the modern German aircraft. They were less heavily armed, they were slower, and they lacked the means even of staying at the same height as the Luftwaffe; Polish fighter pilots were left fuming and helpless while German bombers pulled away from their pursuers.

Against this diminutive Polish Air Force – many of which were destroyed on the ground or rendered useless because of severed communications – the Germans had available something like 1,600 first line machines. Of these the fighter force came to four hundred planes, most of which were Me-109s, with a small number of Me-110 twin-engine fighters, and 'a handful' of Heinkel He-51s – the last biplane in service.

Of all these machines, notes Wing Commander Asher Lee, 'it was the 109 that was the aerial juggernaught, the spearhead of the Luftwaffe.'

It was the effectiveness of the entire Luftwaffe, the fighter force especially, which resulted in German propaganda boasts to the effect that the invasion of Poland was little more than 'a Campaign of Eighteen Days.' This was all true enough. The Me-109s tore the Polish fighter force to shreds and cut the Polish bombers to ribbons, leaving the way open for the Junkers Ju-87 dive bombers, supported by Heinkel He-111 twin-engined bombers and Messerschmitt Me-110 'destroyers', to demoralize the Poles on the ground. It could almost be said that there was no air war over Poland; just an unequal struggle which degenerated into a slaughter.

Nothing better illustrates the effectiveness of the Me-109s in Poland than the situation only a few days after the opening of the German assault. Junkers Ju-52s – tri-motored transports that were normally helpless under fighter attack – droned un-molested over Warsaw, acting as bombers and pouring explosives indiscriminately down on the city. They could do so with impunity, for Me-109s had wiped out the opposition.

By the closing days of 1939 the forces of Germany on one side, and France and England on the other, were girding for full-scale battles. During this 'war of waiting', limited air action was carried out by both sides. and there were several occasions when the Me-109s had the opportunity to try their strength against the British bombers. Several small-scale raids took place and, finally, on the 18th December 1939, a force primarily of Me-109s with some Me-110s in the intercepting group, attacked twenty four twin-engine Wellington bombers near Wilhelmshaven. Twelve Wellingtons went down in the fierce contest and of this number ten fell before the guns of the Me-109E fighters; two Me-109Es were shot down and several others damaged heavily by the defensive fire of the Wellington four-gun tail turrets. In this first major engagement between the British bombers and the German fighters the latter were clearly the victors. Two fighters for the loss of twelve bombers – half the entire attacking force – is enough to discourage any bomber command.

The battle was especially important for another reason. The fighters involved were the new Me-109E-3 models, mounting three cannon and two machine guns of which the third cannon was mounted in the nose, and the value of the additional cannon, firing explosive shells over long range, was evident. Not all German pilots had agreed with its installation in the Me-109E-3, for although the additional weight of firepower was, of course, effective, unfortunately (for the pilots) the engine-mounted cannon often fired with a severe vibration, in some cases so serious as to cause minor damage to the airplane. A number of pilots found this so disconcerting that they refused to use the weapon and relied instead on the normal armament of two cannon in the wings and the two nose guns.

The first Me-109E-3 fighters went into first-line service late in 1939. Numerically, it became the most important fighter in the Luftwaffe

A *rotte* (two aircraft tactical unit) of Me-109E scrambles from a grass airstrip during the opening months of war, when the 109 ruled the sky

An Me-109E cruises above the clouds ready to pounce on any unwary aircraft below

Me-109E-3
Engine: Daimler-Benz 601A, 1,100 hp.
Armament: 2 x 7.9-mm machine guns
and 3 x 20-mm cannon. *Speed:* 354 mph
at 12,300 ft. *Ceiling:* 37,500 ft. *Range:*
412 miles. *Weights:* 4,421 lbs empty and
5,523 lbs loaded. *Span:* 32 ft 4½ ins
Length: 28 ft 3 ins

arsenal with 1,868 aircraft delivered
in 1940, and the production rate by
the close of 1939 had reached approximately one hundred and fifty planes
per month. With the growing demand
for fighters the German factories were,
in fact, hard-pressed to keep the Me-
109E-3s flowing to the front-line units –
yet the German government, yielding
to the need for foreign currency,
signed agreements which called for the
export of 304 Me-109E-3 fighters to other
nations. Bulgaria received nineteen;
Japan two; Rumania sixty nine;
Switzerland eighty; Hungary forty;
Slovakia sixteen; Yugoslavia seventy
three; and Russia five. The two fighters
that went to Japan had been intended
to serve as the basis for Japanese production of the Me-109E-3 by Kawasaki,

but Japanese pilots held the Me-109E-3
in strong disfavour because of its high
wing loading and what they considered
to be poor manoeuverability.

The war moved in fits and starts,
with the German fighter pilots chafing
at the bit to get into action. Germany
moved against Norway on the 8th
April 1940, but those Luftwaffe fighter
pilots expecting sharp action against
their opponents were in for a severe
disappointment. Approximately one
hundred fighters were used by the
Luftwaffe in the Norwegian operation
– seventy long-range Me-110s and
thirty Me-109E-3s – but they saw
little combat. Airpower during the
onslaught against Norway was relegated essentially to a supporting role
– bombers striking at carefully
selected targets and transports carrying troops and supplies.

But on 10th May 1940, a month after
the strikes against Norway were
launched, the Germans moved out in
their massive assault against the
West. German forces ripped into the
stunned defenders of Holland and
moved swiftly against France and the

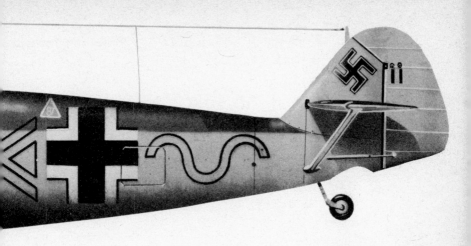

Low Countries; the Flanders Campaign saw about 3,500 German aircraft thrown against the defenders – of which 850 were Me-109s and another 200 to 300 were Me-110s.

There is a dispute about the number of Me-109E-3 fighters that were available at that time. Nowarra, Green, and Windrow, who have all done authoritative works on the Me-109 series, claim that 850 Me-109-E-3 fighters were available, and this means, of course, that all other Me-109E variants had been replaced. This airplane had reached operational service in the last few months of 1939 and had been in production for just over four months of 1940 when the campaign began – so it is difficult to accept that all 850 Me-109s available for the campaign were of the E-3 variant, since production by January of 1940 was just reaching 150 planes a month. A small point, perhaps – but when one considers training, transition, delivery, losses in test and delivery flights, operational attrition, etc., the figure of 850 Me-109E-3 fighters ready for combat does seem open to question.

Detailed historical figures often preserve some room for doubt, but about the effectiveness of the Luftwaffe against its opponents in May 1940 there is no room for argument. The German Air Force, led by the marauding Me-109s, in swift order crushed their opposition and kept the skies secure for German bombers and transports. The onslaught at dawn of the first day of the attack saw the Luftwaffe tearing into Allied airfields, and in Holland the Fokker D.XX1 fighters of the Netherlands Air Force had little opportunity to fight it out with the Me-109s; most of them were wrecked on the ground in the initial attacks. Those Dutch fighters which did get into the air were overwhelmed swiftly by the German pilots flying planes greatly superior to the Fokkers, and in much the same manner the Messerschmitts rampaged through the airfields of Belgium.

Five days after the Germans unleashed the Luftwaffe the Netherlands was broken as a military force with no alternative but to surrender, and thirteen days later the Belgians,

Luftwaffe 'blackmen', as mechanics were known, service the engine of a 109 of II/JG 54 'Grünherz'

their military strength also shattered, followed suit. The initial onslaught was so effective and overwhelming that there was little opportunity for the classical air battles to develop.

It must be noted, however, that the Me-109E had yet to prove itself in the eyes of many airpower strategists. Combat against Dutch, Belgian, or Russian aircraft was not considered the best indicator of the Me-109E's ability, for what was needed, insisted these critics, was a test of the machine against a really outstanding fighter, such as the British Hurricane or Spitfire.

According to claims made at the time, the Hurricane was equal – perhaps superior – to any other fighter plane in the world, but it would seem that this was not true so far as the Me-109E was concerned.

Adolf Galland has stressed this point – which appears to have been ignored by those staunch defenders of Hawker's fighter. 'The Belgians,'

stated Galland, 'for the most part flew antiquated Hurricanes, in which even more experienced pilots could have done little against our new Me-109E. We outstripped them in speed, in rate of climb, in armament and above all in flying experience and training.'

On 12th May 1940 Galland and his wingman made a diving attack against eight Hurricanes. The Germans were in an excellent position at 12,000 feet with the unsuspecting Belgians 9,000 feet below them remaining oblivious of the Germans' approach until Galland was able to get off his first burst without the slightest evasive action from his opponent. 'The poor devil at last noticed what it was all about,' Galland related. 'He took rather clumsy avoiding action which brought him into the fire of my companion. The other seven Hurricanes made no effort to come to the aid of their comrade in distress, but made off in all directions. After a second attack my opponent spun down in spirals minus his rudder. Parts of the wings came off. Another burst would have been a waste of ammu-

Major Adolf Galland, fourth highest scoring Luftwaffe ace in the West, beside his Me-109E with its 'Micky Mouse' personal marking

ition. I immediately went after another of the scattered Hurricanes. This one tried to escape by diving, but I was soon on her tail at a distance of one hundred yards. The Belgium did a half-roll and disappeared through a hole in the clouds. I did not lose track of him and attacked again from very close quarters. The plane zoomed for a second, stalled, and dived vertically to the ground from a height of only ,500 ft.'

France promised to be a different matter. Including all available French single-seat and twin-engined fighters, as well as British Gladiators and Hurricanes, the French could muster for the defense against attacking German forces nearly 800 fighter aircraft, the majority of fighters being the Morane-Saulnier M.S. 406 which made up eleven groups. The Curtiss Hawk 75A equipped another our groups; most pilots preferred the Hawk, with excellent manoeuvera-

bility and rate of climb, to the Morane.

There were some 300 Morane 406 and 100 Hawk 75A machines in first-line service at the outbreak of war, and other fighters included the twin-engined Potez 630 and 631, the Dewoitine D.520, the Bloch 151 and 152, and an assortment of odd machines such as the Dewoitine D.501, Nieuport-Delage 629, and the Bleriot-Spad 510 – none of which were fit to be in the air with the Me-109E. In addition to these aircraft the French received support from two squadrons of Gloster Gladiator biplane fighters and four squadrons of Hawker Hurricanes of the Royal Air Force; immediately after the initial attack by Germany the British threw another six squadrons of Hurricanes into the conflict.

With first light on 10th May 1940 the Luftwaffe struck with stunning effectiveness. German fighters and bombers ripped into the main air bases of Dijon, Lyon, Metz, Nancy and Romilly and from that first strike and for the next six weeks, when the French capitulated, the Germans were never in jeopardy of losing their mastery of the air. Dozens of French

69

A *schwarm* (four aircraft tactical unit) of Me-109Es belonging to I/JG 3 'Udet' patrols over the Channel

fighters and bombers were destroyed during the opening blow.

Until this major assault by the Luftwaffe there had been little air activity between these two combatants. The French scored first blood on 8th September 1939 when five Hawk 75As mixed it up with an equal force of Me-109Es – and shot down two of the Messerschmitts without loss to the French. But from that day until May 10th the battle was contained within the 'wait and prepare' policy of both nations. When the Germans exploded into action it was with a vengeance – and a series of overwhelming victories.

History has obscured the courage and the tenacity with which the French fighter pilots battled the numerically and qualitatively superior enemy. The story has grown that French pilots preferred to abandon their airfields on foot rather than to meet the Germans in the air, but there is little indeed to support such a story and the record shows – and should – that as long as their machines were flyable, most pilots fought to the bitter, predictable end.

Most of the French pilots flew aircraft outclassed in almost every respect by the Me-109E-3 and the men who flew the more modern French fighters had had precious little time in which to become fully experienced in their machines. Ground communication was a shambles, attack warning almost non-existent, and efficient utilization of air-ground defenses a joke. Dozens of brand-new fighter planes were left, worthless to the battle, in reserve airfields because they lacked gunsights or propellers or other equipment necessary to fit them out as fighting machines while in the forward areas those fields within range of the Luftwaffe were exposed to a merciless and relentless beating from the air. Allied pilots ran short of ammunition, fuel, and supplies, a situation known to German Intelli-

gence and of which the command took every advantage.

By the time of the Dunkirk evacuation, it seemed that the German army was moving so swiftly on the ground that panic-stricken French troops and supply units hastily set aflame vast stocks of fuel and ammunition – and French pilots often found themselves landing on airfields already set afire and abandoned by their own men. Out of fuel, lacking needed parts, the pilots had no choice but to abandon their machines as German ground units closed in on the fields.

The details of the air battles have for the most part been lost, but an idea of their magnitude may be gained by the fact that the Luftwaffe lost approximately 350 aircraft during the six-weeks campaign. Most of these losses were claimed by French fighter pilots who, in the confusion of battle, registered claims for 684 confirmed kills as well as 251 probables. Luftwaffe statistics indicate, however, that no more than 350 German aircraft were lost to all causes.

The end of this short war was a time for serious reflection. Despite isolated incidents where French fighters triumphed, the Me-109E had swept the field of all opposition, and even the alleged manoeuverability of the French fighters had proven inferior to that of the Me-109E, which met the enemy under all possible conditions.

Even more of a shock was the vulnerability of the Hurricane to the Me-109E. As much as the French fighters involved, the Hurricane was outclassed in almost every respect by the Me-109E and one of the facts of the air war for France in 1940 that is not widely known is that during the brief aerial conflict the British lost approximately 450 Hurricane fighters – with, it should be added, distressingly little effect upon German air operations.

Above: The 109s had air superiority but were not invincible. Here one brought down by French anti-aircraft fire is guarded by a French soldier

Below: An Me-109E comes in for a mock attack in December 1939. Note the wingman ready to protect his leader's tail if he is attacked

Me-109E versus Spitfire

Which was the better fighter in air-to-air combat – the Messerschmitt or the Spitfire? This was the question which dominated the minds of world leaders during the hot, crucial summer of 1940. The answer demands specified circumstances. At this point in the 'character study' of the Me-109 the question must relate to the Me-109E-3 and E-4 as against the merits of the Spitfire 1 and II, since these were the principal antagonists during the Battle of Britain. The date most often accepted as commencing the Battle of Britain is August 13th, 1940 and the time when it ended, again – as a matter of common agreement, is during May of 1941. What is of prime interest to us is the performance of the Me-109E during that time.

During the early phases of the Battle of Britain the German fighter used both for bomber escort and for 'sweep and destroy' missions was the Me-109E-3, which has already been described. As the fighting continued

An escort patrol of Me-109Es protects bombers over the Channel

the improved Me-109E-4 came into service, with first-line Luftwaffe units, and the differences between the E-3 and E-4 models are slight but pertinent to this story. Armor protection for the pilot was improved and pilot visibility bettered. There were other minor changes to the aircraft, but its basic change was in armament, for complaints about the engine-mounted cannon in the E-3 model had become so widespread that the weapon was removed from the E-4 subvariant and this airplane went into service with two nose guns and two wing-mounted MG FF 20-mm cannon. The nose guns each had 1,000 rounds of ammunition and the wing cannon each had 60 rounds of explosive shell. Empty weight was 4,440 lbs and the gross 5,520 lbs. Fuel was carried in a fuselage tank, with a maximum capacity of eighty eight gallons. The DB-601A engine was rated at 1,150 hp at 2,400 RPM for takeoff, the maximum speed was slightly higher than the Me-109E-3 and rated at 357 mph. Other performance approximated to that of the earlier subvariant.

Prior to the 'official' opening of the Battle of Britain with the launching of heavy bomber raids against England on 13th August 1940, formations of Me-109E-3 fighters had been over the English Channel flying patrols and looking for targets of opportunity. It should be stressed that the pilots flew two or three sorties per day, clear testimonial to the reliability and serviceability of the machine, for the strains of takeoffs, climb to altitude, and the various loads of flight are considerably greater than for a single mission of equal duration. During this period the Germans began to engage with greater frequency the Spitfire, an airplane of which they had heard much and which was to have an impact, unpleasant and often lethal, among the Me-109 forces. If their experience against the Hurricane gave the Germans much reason for rejoicing, those German pilots who felt the Spitfire could be included in the same category soon had their complacency shattered.

These early raids against English objectives also brought a growing confirmation of the most serious deficiency of the Me-109E – a range far less than was needed in the heavy air assaults against the British. Already, in the war on the Continent it had been necessary to advance the forward airfields used by the Me-109E in order to remain in contact with the retreating enemy – and only efficient German support organizations on the ground had kept the Messerschmitts effectively in action – but it was a clumsy method of sustaining fighter forces in the field.

A greater endurance and range built into the Me-109E would have eased tremendously the loads imposed upon Luftwaffe logistics and what appears surprising, in 20–20 hindsight vision, is that the Germans did not make immediate use of external fuel tanks that could be jettisoned just prior to entering combat. The Japanese, faced with the need for long-range fighters, solved their problem neatly with disposable tanks for their Zero fighters which, at the beginning of the war, were the longest-ranging fighters of any air force in the world.

Certainly the Germans recognized the need for long-range performance in the Me-109E. The fact that many British target areas were beyond the range of the Me-109E meant that German bombers arrived over target without fighter escort, and there seems no question but that the short range of the Me-109E – never corrected for the critical engagements with the Royal Air Force – was one of the major factors in the disastrous defeat suffered by the Luftwaffe, a defeat that was one of the turning points of the entire war.

The Me-109E fighters never had more than twenty minutes' combat time in which to protect their bombers against intercepting British fighters. Had the Me-109E been able to gain only thirty ninutes' more time in the combat area then the Battle of Britain might have been won by a margin even narrower than that recorded by history.

It must be stressed that the short range of the Me-109E was not an insoluble problem, and that in fact, it could have been corrected with comparative technological ease and with little burden upon either German industry or the Luftwaffe.

The failure to do so was an error of incalculable proportion.

On the 15th August 1940 the British showed their steel in massive air battles that resulted in the combat loss of seventy five German planes at a cost of thirty four British planes, and many other Luftwaffe fighters and bombers were so heavily damaged that they either failed to return to base or were later written off as wrecks beyond economical repair. The 15th August was a day of reckoning in yet another manner. Formations of Junkers Ju-87 Stukas, the dive bombers so dreaded for their performance in Europe, were torn apart by the British fighters, and in addition Norwegian-based strike forces of the Luftwaffe, unescorted by German fighters, also suffered severe losses to the intercepting RAF fighters. The battles of this day opened a three-week period during which the fighting waxed with a fury unprecedented in aerial conflict.

Above: A pilot of III/JG 51 'Moelders' scrambles aboard his aircraft. *Below:* An Me-109E taxies out for take off in September 1940

Pilots try to relax as they wait for the next mission

Mechanics make last-minute checks as the pilot puts on his mask

42 victory bars on the rudder show this to be the mount of an ace

Mechanics work to get a 109E back into the air for its next mission

The Germans did not try to avoid the Spitfire and Hurricanes; on the contrary, it was their intention to draw the British fighters into a battle, where the attrition of aerial fighting, even on a one-to-one basis with the Messerschmitts, would have broken the back of the British fighter defense. Simultaneously with these great air battles the Luftwaffe hammered at British airfields. Biggin Hill and Manston especially took a severe mauling and, had the Germans not switched suddenly on 7th September to amount their assault against London directly, the British Fighter Command would have found itself in a state of near collapse. Indeed, plans had already been made to remove all fighter forces from the airfields south of London; they were to be flown to the north of London where they would be beyond the reach of the Me-109E fighters.

It is not generally realized just how effective were the Me-109Es during the

A *schwarm* of Me-109Es climbing on their way toward the British coast

Battle of Britain. Only their lack of range (or time spent over target) forced German pilots to break off fighting many times when conditions favored them.

The early plans for the campaign against England had called for Me-110 twin-engine fighters to escort German bombers on long range missions. But the Me-110, despite high speed and a powerful armament, was itself highly vulnerable to British fighters (British and later American pilots referred to Me-110s as 'meat on the table' because of their inability to stand up to Allied fighter attacks). As a consequence Me-109Es were forced to escort and defend the Me–110 fighters! The Ju-87s were so open to destruction by the British Hurricanes and Spitfires that they too required fighter protection – and fighters are effective on strike missions only when they can be cut free from the bombers to attack the defenders under the best possible conditions to the escorting planes.

There is no question but that in the 'reef it in tight' in vertical turns the Spitfire was superior to the Me-

109E. That is of great importance in fighter-vs-fighter combat but by no means is it an overwhelming factor, as has been shown countless times in combat between the Me-109E and the Spitfire or, for that matter, between such combatants as the Zero *vs* the Corsair. There are too many other factors that influence the outcome of a fighter struggle.

'Official' performance figures give the Spitfire 1 a maximum speed of 367 mph and the Me-109E of 354 mph. Such figures should always be held in some suspicion since they are affected by the condition of the engine, temperature, altitude, surface condition of the aircraft, weight of the pilot, and other factors.

It is still believed that the Spitfire 1 was faster than the Me-109E. Yet almost every German pilot involved in fights with the Spitfire insisted that the Me-109E was the faster airplane. Galland, for example, makes the point that the Spitfire, faster than the Hurricane, was 'slower than our planes by about ten to fifteen mph but could perform steeper and tighter turns. The older Hawker Hurricane compared badly with our Me-109 as regards speed and rate of climb.'

Another factor was that the British engines used carburetors rather than the direct fuel injection of the Daimler-Benz in the Me-109E. This seemingly minor difference was of vital importance, for in inverted attitudes the British engine was likely to sputter and lose power – extremely disturbing to say the least, in the midst of a dogfight! As Galland put it the German 'engines had injection pumps instead of the carburetors used by the British, and therefore they did not conk out through lack of acceleration in critical moments during combat. The British fighters usually tried to shake off pursuit by a half-roll or half-roll on top of a loop, while we simply went straight for them, with wide-open throttle and eyes bulging out of our sockets'.

Galland's 'summary judgement' of the two airplanes was that 'the Me-109 was superior in the attack and not so suitable for purely defensive purposes as the Spitfire, which, although a little

slower, was much more manoeuver-able.'

Reviewing events of the time, Galland records that two or three missions per day was normal for the Luftwaffe pilots and that often their mission orders would read: 'Free chase over southeast England.' Most entries into British airspace on such sorties, Galland related, were usually carried out between 21,000 and 24,000 feet. From takeoff to arrival over England, crossing at the narrowest part of the Channel, required some thirty minutes. With thirty minutes' flying time to return this gave a 'free chase' of only twenty minutes which the German pilots considered grossly inadequate. Galland pointed out that they could 'barely cover the south-eastern parts of the British Isles ... Everything beyond was practically out of our reach. This was the most acute weakness of our offensive. An operating radius of one hundred and twenty five miles was sufficient for local defense, but not enough for such tasks as were now demanded of us.'

Heinz Knoke in a report of combat with Spitfires complained that the 'bastards can make such infernally tight turns; there seems to be no way of nailing them. Grunert spends several minutes trying to catch two of the Tommies flying close together; but they always break away and vanish into the overcast.'

Johannes Steinhof, veteran of the Battle of Britain fighting, felt that in the early fighting 'the 109 had a certain advantage, except for its turning radius, but the later Spitfire had a higher ceiling and better climb.'

RAF pilot Al Deere who flew the Spitfire II (which differed from the Mark I through use of a constant-speed propeller) felt that, in a comparison of Spitfire vs Hurricane, the latter was a 'better gun platform and there-fore more effective against bombers, but it could not have lived without Spitfires to take on the 109s, whereas the Spitfires could have lived without the Hurricanes.'

Jeffrey Quill was a Spitfire test pilot who also fought against the attacking Me-109s: 'It was certainly necessary to pull out all the stops in order to fight the 109, but at altitude we had the edge on them and they treated the Spitfire with respect.'

M V Blake, comparing the Spitfire with the Me-109E, described the British fighter as 'a precision instrument; it and the 109 were so close that the chap who had the height advantage would be the victor.'

Steinhof and Galland offer some parting shots in after-the-war evaluations of the Hurricane vs the Me-109E. 'The Hurricane,' said Steinhof, 'was a big disadvantage to you [British], the rate of roll being bad – we were lucky to meet Hurricanes.'

Galland put it more bluntly: 'The Hurricane was hopeless – a nice airplane to shoot down.'

Alexander McKee in *Strike From the Sky* refers to the Hurricane's poor performance above 18,000 ft and comments that the 109 pilots always grasped every opportunity to hit the Hurricanes in diving attacks. McKee writes: 'Malinowski was three times with formations which were jumped on from the top: the first time, he was shot down; the second time, the attackers consisted only of six 109s but they got two Hurricanes as they dived through; the third time, there was only one 109, but he also shot down two Hurricanes.'

McKee makes reference to October of 1940 when the combat moved as high as 30,000 feet, and when it became 'a hard time for the pilots of the unheated Hurricanes, whose best performance was below 18,000 feet; frozen, dazed with cold, they hauled their soggy aircraft up under the high-flying Messerschmitts. Only the Spitfires could fight on even terms.'

History, which has recorded the disastrous failure of the Luftwaffe in the Battle of Britain, sometimes obscures the fact that the battle was not won through a continuous and overwhelming destruction of German aircraft with only limited British loss. At times quite the contrary was the case, as McKee illustrates so well: 'In the week beginning on 31st August and ending on 6th September, Fighter Command lost 161 fighters in air battles alone, against a German loss of 154 bombers and fighters. The battle in the air – of fighter versus fighter – was

An Me-109E dives down to attack British fighters still on their climb

Me-109Es over the Channel, where
many were forced to ditch on their way
home because of shortage of fuel

Below: A good shot of an Me-109E-1 in the early pattern camouflage. *Bottom:* Me-109Es silhouetted against an evening sky on their way to England

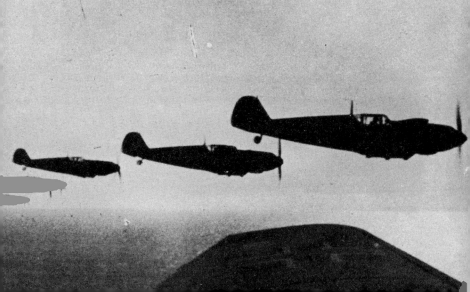

being decisively won by the Luftwaffe. If this continued, there really would be no British fighters left, or at any rate not enough to put up an effective defense . . .'

Martin C Windrow, who has written an excellent accounting of the Me-109E series, provides the summation that while the Hurricane clearly was inferior to the Me-109E the Spitfire was another matter and 'Mitchell's tight-turning thoroughbred soon earned the profound respects of the Messerschmitt pilots. The technical advantages and disadvantages largely cancelled each other out when the Bf 109E was pitted against the Spitfire; the outcome of any dogfight depended to a great extent on the skill and determination of the pilots . . .'

Roland P Beaumont of England, reviewing a book about fighter pilots, written by the American author (and fighter pilot, also) Edward Sims, had these extremely pertinent remarks to make – 'In his assessment of the equipment involved in the Battle of Britain the author produces an accurate summary of the qualities of the Me-109, Spitfire, and Hurricane, but concludes that the 109 had the edge of performance over both the British aircraft and although the latter were more manoeuverable, the Me-109 comes out as the best machine of the time'.

This understates the case for the British aircraft, because the direct comparison which one was able to make when testing captured enemy aircraft during the latter part of the war, showed without question that with its seriously restricted vision, poor ground stability and positively frightful lateral control in the dive, characteristics which were mitigated but not out-weighed by heavier armament and fuel-injected negative 'g' power advantages, the 109 was in some ways an inferior fighting aeroplane in comparison with both Spitfire and Hurricane. To fly a 109 once would have been the best boost to morale that a British fighter could have had at that time, had he needed it! . . .

Obviously Galland, Steinhof and others who flew the Me-109E – to say nothing of British pilots who opposed the airplane – are at odds with Mr Beaumont; but it is the sort of argument that will never end in agreement of all concerned. What is clear is that by any yardstick the Me-109E, on the basis of fighter-*vs*-fighter, took a back seat to no other machine then in the air. Despite Mr. Beaumont's defense of the Hurricane as against the Me-109E, the results of repeated combats showed clearly, as RAF pilot Al Deere noted, that the Hurricane 'could not have lived without Spitfires to take on the 109s . . .'

Those pilots (on both sides) who flew the Me-109E were unanimous that despite any shortcomings it was an excellent fighting machine. At low speeds its control response was a delight to the pilot. Above speeds of 350 mph, however, the Me-109E's controls became inordinately heavy (German pilots agreed with this), and by the time 400 mph was reached, moving the ailerons demanded extraordinary strength and rolling manoeuvers were beyond the capacity of the average pilot. Yet the Me-109E, at low or high speeds, had both an excellent angle and rate of climb, and it could fly and fight at altitudes beyond the reach of the Spitfires which it opposed. Above 20,000 feet the Me-109E was generally accepted as the better machine, although there are isolated voices to contest that conclusion.

The Messerschmitt could be 'slammed' into a vertical dive from level flight. Normally such a manoeuver in combat was suicide, but so rapid was the acceleration and so swift the dive that this manoeuver often saved the lives of German pilots caught in unfavorable situations with the British (the advantage was lost when the Messerschmitt faced the Thunderbolt and the Mustang). There was one other disadvantage to the Me-109E which is not reflected in statistical portraits of performance. The pilot had no means of trimming the rudder from the cockpit. Most pilots felt this a major fault in the Me-109E, for during a fast dive the rudder became quite heavy and difficult to move – and then reversed trim, demanding much of the pilot who found fatigue a problem after long minutes of combat.

One of the more revealing commentaries on the Messerschmitt was provided in the official report of a British pilot who, during the Battle of

Britain, had the opportunity to test a captured Me-109E. In his report the pilot stated, after first examining the machine on the ground, that the manufacturer had provided 'an aerodynamic finish superior to contemporary British aircraft – for the inset juncture of slat trailing edges with the wings, and the close fit and straightness of the flap shroud and slot, were superb.'

Regarding the dangerous landing attitude of the Me-109E, the British pilot reports: 'When I came to fly the machine its steep landing attitude showed the snag I expected. The tendency was to make a wheel landing, since the aeroplane had to be rotated through a bigger angle than one was accustomed with machines of similar vintage such as Spitfires, Hurricanes, and Curtiss Hawks. It required deliberate mental effort to pull the stick further back than the attitude which normally gave the stall; but if the movement was checked at what seemed a safe point, the Me-109 played a fast one by dropping its left wing just before touchdown. If, however, Lysander technique was used, rumbling the machine in at a steep attitude, it would sink gently to the ground in a perfect three-pointer – a method which at first appears unsafe, but one to which a pilot quickly becomes accustomed, and then the behaviour of conventional aeroplanes seems wrong!'

The test pilot felt the 'cockpit was cramped' and that the 'windscreen was like a tunnel, for it was made with a flat front portion to which were attached, by broad frames, large flat side-panels, the top being boxed in with a curved roof.' The pilot reported unfavorably on rear vision, and found that the armor plating that protected the pilot's head also 'tapped my skull as the machine taxied across the bumpy aerodrome. The cockpit enclosure, however . . . excelled among all other aircraft I had flown . . . in the complete absence of draught from its clear vision opening . . . In the dirty weather conditions under which the test was made this proved invaluable. Though rain at times made the windscreen opaque, I could see ahead whatever the speed of the Me-109. In Hurricane or Spitfire it would have been necessary to throttle back and open

the hood . . .' The pilot felt the cockpit was much too narrow and that bailing out of the machine might prove difficult. On the positive side of things he found 'the rest of the cockpit layout was excellent' and that the 'control column grip came nicely to hand, the single lever, gateless throttle was delightfully straightforward . . . the juxtaposition of wheel controls for flap operation and tailplane was excellent . . .'

When he 'opened up the engine' he found that its 'response to the throttle was instantaneous. However fast the lever was opened or shut there was no sign of choking. Definitely a good point for direct-injection, I thought . .'

What about those terrible tendencies of the Me-109E during takeoff? The report continues: '. . . the throttle was pushed steadily forward. Once again there was an impression made by the perfect pick-up of the engine; and then the aeroplane began to move. *There was no hasty jamming of rudder to counteract the heavy swing often found with single-engined fighters* [Italics Added], and the tail lifted firmly and cleanly when the stick was held well forward. The view improved, though it was still far from good. Quickly the little fighter accelerated, its rather stiff undercarriage imposing a slight lateral rocking as the wheels bounced across the turf.

'Pilots had told me that if the Me was pulled off the ground the moment flying speed was sufficient, the port wing would not lift, even though the machine was vitually airborne. Applying opposite stick would lift the wing momentarily, ailerons would snatch gently from side to side, and the wing would drop again. Since the flow over the wing at low speed seemed critical – perhaps owing to hunting of the slots, for they had no dampers – I held the machine down for a few seconds longer than was necessary. Despite that, the takeoff was surprisingly short; the aeroplane left the ground sweetly, and slanted up at a rate of climb which would have beaten a competing Spitfire.'

During the ensuing flight, after spending some time manoeuvering the airplane – although any pilot wants more than one flight in which to become acquainted with his machine –

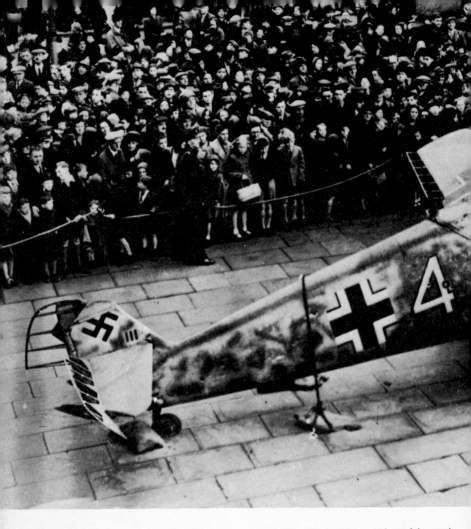

An Me-109E, which has made a belly-landing during the Battle, on display at Bolton in Lancashire to raise funds and boost morale

the British pilot was given the opportunity to put the Me-109E through its paces when a Spitfire joined up with the German fighter. The pilot in the Messerschmitt watched the Spitfire coming closer until 'it was alongside with its broad wing tucked between mine and the tail. The pilot grinned and jerked a thumb. I pulled back on the stick, and laughed to see the Spit shoot underneath as the little Messerschmitt stood on its tail and climbed steeply away.

'In an endeavor to retrieve his position the Spitfire pilot climbed steeply, but it only resulted in placing himself in a position where I could make a short dive for his tail. I jammed the nose down so hard that a Spitfire or Hurricane doing the same manoeuvre would have choked its engine, but the direct-injection system did not even falter. Gun sights could only be held momentarily on the Spitfire; then he did a flick half roll and was off in a steep dive with a change of direction which the Me-109 could not quickly follow.

'For a few minutes we climbed, twisted and dived after each other. It was an interesting contest. Many

times the steep climbing attitude of the German machine would evade the Spitfire, and the abruptness with which the nose could be thrust down had its undoubted advantage. Yet when it came to manoeuvring at speed, although the Spitfire lateral control of those days was not good, the heavy weight of the Messerschmitt's controls proved not only exhausting but impossible. Aileron could only be applied slowly, and so the response was slow; the best one could do was to evade the Spitfire by gentle turns at very low speed and then strike him down by cunning. Tighten these turns to 4g and the machine began to drop out of the sky after a preparatory warning flick caused by the opening of the slats. However, the behaviour even then was excellent, for no spin resulted, and normal flight was instantly regained by easing the backward pressure on the stick.'

'Whether the Me's advantage was more apparent than real could only be settled by consensus of opinion, for the radius of turn in practice depends not so much on aerodynamic characteristics as the extent to which a pilot is prepared to approach the stall. Possibly the Spitfire pilot could have pulled a little harder and thus followed my machine around, but I fancy the slats did in fact give the Messerschmitt a slight advantage.'

Improving the breed

While the Battle of Britain stormed to its disastrous conclusion for the Luftwaffe, Messerschmitt engineers were hard at work producing a series of subvariants of the Me-109E to meet the demands of special combat conditions. The bomb rack which had been first used with the Me-109E-1/B was fitted to the E-4 model to produce the Me-109E-4/B version. Another subvariant of the E-4 was the 109E-4/N which received the new DB-601N engine of 1,200 hp, featuring improved fuel injection and a super-charger drive with automatically-controlled hydraulic coupling. Most of the E-4/N versions were sent to bear the brunt of fighting in North Africa for which the airplane was further modified to resist the effects of desert sand and dust. The E-4/N also was fitted out with bomb racks for ground support missions. (Many of the Me-109E, F and G series, while not specifically designated as fighter-bombers, received field modifications which enabled them to carry drop tanks, bombs, and other weapons.)

Five specific subvariants remained in the Me-109E series. The E-5 and E-6 had their armament reduced to only the two nose guns for conversion to short-range reconnaissance aircraft. In some versions the radio set was also removed to accommodate the camera equipment. The E-5 was powered with the DB-601A and the E-6 with the DB-601N engine, otherwise the two aircraft were identical.

The range shortcomings of the E-3 and E-4 fighters in the Battle of Britain received a belated solution with the E-7 which was a basic E-4 fighter modified to carry a single jettisonable belly tank of sixty six-gallons (Imperial) fuel. E-7 models were used throughout the Mediterranean – where they sometimes fought Me-109E-3 fighters flown by Yugoslavian pilots! A further modification took place when the E-7 was modified to fill a ground

Top: In an attempt to increase the 109's offensive capabilities, Hitler ordered that a certain number of aircraft in each *Geschwader* should carry bombs. *Bottom:* Another failing remedied – an extra fuel tank under the fuselage

Me-109E-4/Ns in North Africa
with JG 26

Better equipment to support the Afrika Korps – the Me-109F-2/Trop

attack role. Designated Me-109E-7/U2 (the U representing modification); the airplane received additional armor plating to protect the coolant radiators and the engine from ground fire, and saw its greatest service in North Africa. A special engine modification distinguished the Me-109E-7/Z model; the engine was fitted with nitrous oxide injection into the supercharger to improve high-altitude characteristics.

The E-8 was a 'catch up' model which included in its manufacture the many improvements and modifications of the previous aircraft. The engine was the DB-601E of 1,200 hp. The last of the E line was the E-9 model, another fighter reconnaissance machine with two guns and heavy camera installation.

There was one another major innovation in the E series, however, the Me-109T – only shipboard fighter of World War II produced by Germany

(the T represents Traeger, or, carrier), and intended for use aboard the *Graf Zeppelin*, which never reached active duty. Fieseler modified ten E-3 airframes by increasing the wingspan, modifying the wings for manual folding, installing arrestor hooks and catapult spools, fitting spoilers to the upper surface of the wings (to steepen the approach and shorten the landing run) and installing locking tailwheels. When work on the carrier was abandoned the 109T models had their special equipment removed and, with the increased wingspan and locking tailwheels, were assigned to duty in

Norway.

That was the last of the E variants, except for Me-109E, Number 5604, which was to start the new line – the Me-109F.

The 'new look' in the Me-109F-series fighter came from a drastically redesigned, symmetrical engine cowling and other external modifications intended to clean up the airplane for better performance. Messerschmitt engineers placed a new supercharger intake further out from the engine mount in order to increase its 'ram air effect.' They enlarged the propeller spinner and reduced the propeller

The sleeker, strutless design of the Me-109F-1 shows clearly in this aircraft of III/JG 54 'Grünherz' whose tail shows the scars of battle

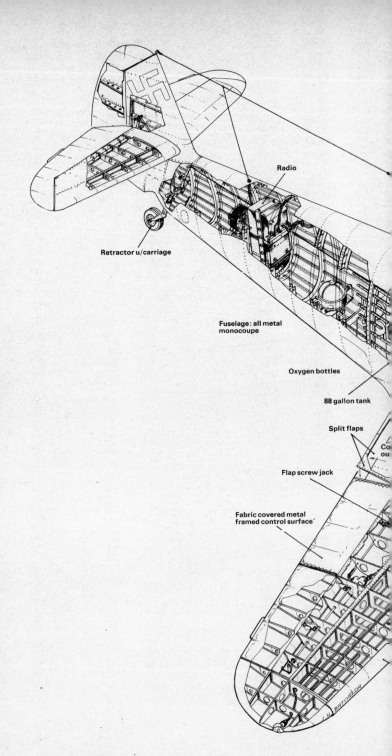

Radio

Retractor u/carriage

Fuselage: all metal
monocoupe

Oxygen bottles

88 gallon tank

Split flaps

Flap screw jack

Fabric covered metal
framed control surface

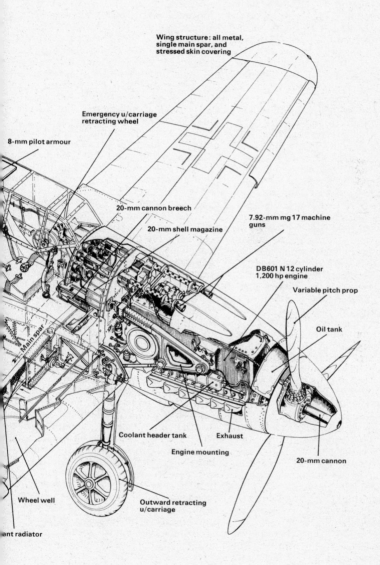

Wing structure: all metal,
single main spar, and
stressed skin covering

Emergency u/carriage
retracting wheel

8-mm pilot armour

20-mm cannon breech

20-mm shell magazine

7.92-mm mg 17 machine
guns

DB601 N 12 cylinder
1,200 hp engine

Variable pitch prop

Oil tank

Main spar

Coolant header tank

Engine mounting

Exhaust

20-mm cannon

Wheel well

Outward retracting
u/carriage

ant radiator

diameter by six inches. Further to enhance streamlining they rebuilt the horizontal tailplane into a cantilever structure and eliminated the external bracing. Drag was reduced still further by designing the underwing radiators in a 'flatter' configuration. On 10th July 1940 the experimental prototype of the new 109F series made its first test flight and hastened the planned replacement of the 109E-series fighter.

By late 1940 the first pre-production Me-109F-0 fighters were being evaluated at test centers by German Air Force pilots. The airplane had been changed even more than the modified 109E/- 5604 which initiated the new design, for the pre-production F-0 models had a new wing of increased span and wingtips slightly more rounded out than the E models. The slotted ailerons were gone, as were the slotted flaps, the latter replaced by standard flaps of reduced size and area.

By January 1941 the first production aircraft, designed Me-109E-1, were in the hands of operational units. Plans to use a more powerful engine than the 1,200 hp DB-601N were shelved because of engine production problems; with the same engine as the latter 109E models, the 109F-1 had a maximum speed of 369 mph at 19,700 feet and an improved service ceiling of 37,700 ft.

Shortly after it entered service the 109F-1 was regarded with misgivings by its pilots. In February of 1941 three pilots, in separate incidents, made frantic radio calls that the airplane was vibrating violently, and before the pilots could bail out, the machines dove out of control into the ground. Several weeks later a 109F-1 lost the entire tail assembly in flight, and engineers studying the wreckage discovered the cause of the vibration, which built up between the engine and the tail, causing the latter to fail. With the modifications made as a result of these studies the problem was considered solved.

Despite the many improvements in the basic design of the fighter, the Me-109F-1 was received with still further reservations, which centered about the new policy of armament. Rather than increasing, or at the least retaining the armament of the E versions, the F series when it went into duty had a marked *decrease* in

firepower. Initially, and through almost the entire production, wing armament was omitted from the airplane, which went into service with two MG 17 nose guns and a single cannon firing through the propeller hub.

'Mixed emotions' suggests in a kindly fashion the reception offered the fighter. Some pilots, such as Werner Moelders, favored the lighter armament which added manoeuverability to the airplane and demanded the pilot exercise better aim than simply spraying bullets and cannon shells at his opponent – but for the most part the lightweight armament provoked howls of dismay from the veterans. Major Walter Oesau was so incensed with what he considered a disastrous move by the Luftwaffe that he refused to fly his F-series fighter while his mechanics had enough spares to keep his 109E-4 in the air. Adolph Galland protested bitterly about what he called an inexplicably retrogressive step; where heavier firepower was needed, the Me-109 F-1 reduced what should have been increased. An attempt to increase the rate and weight of the firepower of the fighter was made in the Me-109F-2, wherein the former 20-mm nose cannon was replaced with 15-mm MG 151 which, because of a better trajectory and higher velocity improved materially the 'on target' ability of the airplane. More than one Luftwaffe fighter pilot, echoing the sentiments of Galland, muttered darkly that emergency fixes would have to be made to compensate for the decision to use the Me-109F as a rapier rather than a heavy sword.

The argument waged hotly for many months to come. The new Spitfire V had made its appearance by this time and the Me-109E fighters were hard-pressed to meet the improved British fighter on even terms. The Me-109F-1 and -2 fighters, however, with improved handling at almost all speeds and with better altitude performance, were considered, in fighting at great heights, to be superior to the Spitfire V.

New subvariants appeared quickly.

Top: An Me-109F-2 of III/JG 3 'Udet' in Russia. *Bottom:* Me109F-3s. The lighter armament was not popular.

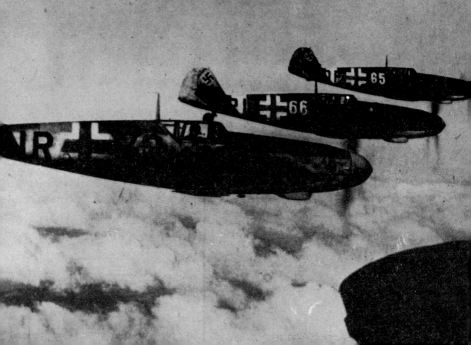

The Me-109F-5 was
a reconnaissance aircraft with only two
guns in the engine cowling

Me-109F-4/R1 with underwing cannon

Originally the F series was to have been powered with the DB-601E engine of 1,300 horsepower but the airplane had to be issued to operational units with the engine that had powered the Me-109E fighters because of delays in getting the DB-601E into production. To compensate for this lack of expected power the Me-109F-2/Z was equipped with power-boosting equipment. The Me-109F-2/Tropical was modified to meet the needs of North African conditions; the engine was protected by special air intake filters and the airplane was equipped with an emergency survival pack for a pilot forced down in the desert.

The majority of Me-109F fighters

then in operational service had been earmarked for the most critical of all German operations, the invasion on the 22nd June 1941 of the Soviet Union. Every attempt was made to bring the F-1 and F-2 airplanes to the Russian front to support this greatest of all invasions, but several *staffels* were still equipped with the Me-109E-4 series when the attack was launched.

The year 1942 with the continued attempts to improve the basic Me-109 design, marked the most profound changes in the airplane. The Me-109F-3, which at last appeared early in 1942, had the DB-601E engine of 1,300 hp and the airplane now performed as its designers had intended. The maximum speed at 22,000 ft was 390 mph, the service ceiling nearly 38,000 ft and the normal cruise range of 440 miles was

achieved with a cruising speed of 310 mph at 16,500 ft. The average empty weight was 4,330 lbs and the normal gross 6,054 lbs. At high altitude especially the Me-109F-3 was an outstanding performer, but its high wing loading of 34.8 lbs per sq ft handicapped it seriously in dogfighting manoeuvers with the Spitfire V. The Me-109 remained, as Galland had remarked long before, still the best fighter for attack, and the Spitfire the best machine for area defense.

The remainder of the F-series were all powered with the DB-601E engine of 1,300 hp. The Me-109F-4 differed only in armament, the 15-mm nose cannon replaced with the new MG 151 cannon of 20-mm. The 109F-4/B was a fighter-bomber version and the 109F-4Trop another modified version for desert conditions.

As many pilots had predicted earlier the Me-109F-4/R1 was the first overt admission of inadequate armament in the F series. The airplane was modified to take a power boosting system in the engine rather than the cannon, and the wing was fitted with underwing racks to mount four RZ 65 rocket projectiles, which could be used either for aerial combat or against ground targets. The R/1 modification slipped quickly into obscurity when armament difficulties forced Messerschmitt to concentrate on more promising possibilities.

Long-range armed reconnaissance was the mission for the 109F-5, while its successor, the 109F-6, carried heavier camera equipment in place of removed armament. Both the F-5 and

F-6 airplanes flew normally between 35,000 and 40,000 ft; their service ceiling with full gross weight at takeoff and climb directly to altitude was 39,400 ft.

The problem of inadequate armament returned full circle to the Me-109F-1 when this fighter was thrown into battles against the increasingly dangerous raids by American heavy bombers. In combat with the B-17s and B-24s the two nose guns and single cannon proved woefully ineffective. Field modifications added a 20-mm MG 151 cannon in a gondola attachment beneath each wing to increase the firepower to two guns and three cannon, and by more than doubling the Me-109F-1 armament the fighter increased its effectiveness against the heavy bombers; at the same time, however, the sudden imposition of weight and drag compromised severely the ability of the Me-109F-1 to defend itself against American escort fighters. In the opening months of the heavy bomber operations the problem arose only rarely, but as the P-38s, P-47s and then P-51s appeared with long-range tanks, the Me-109F-1 and other fighters with doubled armament found themselves sorely beset by the enemy machines. This was to be the most critical problem facing the modified F models, and the G series which followed.

The F-5 and F-6 were the last of the production-line in the Me-109F series, but a number of the F airplanes saw extensive modification as testbeds for other designs. Messerschmitt engineers redesigned the wing of one airplane with boundary layer fences in order to compare the airplane's performance with these fences rather than the Handley-Page slots along the leading edge but apparently there was little in the test results to justify abandoning the original slots design. Messerschmitt now proposed a high-altitude reconnaissance version to be known as the Me-109H, and for preliminary tests the company modified a standard Me-109F airframe to take an experimental wing of greatly increased span. Another F airframe was fitted with the BMW 801 radial engine to compare the Me-109F's

The F series shown to perfection – a clean, sleek design

performance with this powerplant against the Focke-Wulf FW-190, normally powered by the BMW. The result was an 'interesting' machine but the combination of bulky engine with the slim lines of the Me-109F fuselage proved incompatible. The airflow across the tail was extremely turbulent and the airplane could barely be controlled in manoeuvers by its pilot.

Other designs included engine experiments; modifications to the airplane for tricycle landing gear, for which tests were carried out with single and double nosewheels; and experiments for a high-speed long-range fighter and a proposed Messerschmitt bomber. The fighter design was the Me-109Z, built as the prototype of the Me-609, and for these tests engineers mated two Me-109F fuselages and engines to form a single twin-boomed airplane. They mated the left and right wings with a special center section, and joined the vertical tails with a high horizontal stabilizer, but the completed test aircraft, the Me-109Z, never flew. (That the concept was sound received proof years later when North American Aviation carried out the same project with two P-51D fighters, which were integrated into the F-82 Twin Mustang, a swift long-range fighter that went into operational service in several theaters. During its career the F-82 set a world's nonstop distance record, and, was the first American fighter to shoot down Russian fighters in the Korean War).

The bomber design proposed by Messerschmitt was the Me-264 four-engined machine for long-range missions. The first Me-264 proposals included the Vee, or butterfly tail (as on the Beech Bonanza). The Me-109F-4 production aircraft, 14003, was modified with a scaled-down version of the Me-264-design Vee tail. Reduced drag brought about higher speeds but there were so many problems created by this installation that the project was abandoned.

Except for the F-5 and F-6 reconnaissance versions, production of the Me-109F phases out in 1942; during 1941 Germany built a total of 2,628 109E and 109F machines.

Its replacement was the new Me-109G series – which were to make up seventy percent of all Me-109 fighter production.

Gustav VI: 'the killer'

The Me-109G – or Gustav, as it was called by its pilots – represented the most critical phase in the history of the airplane. By May of 1942, when the first G models went into production, the 109 design had reached the zenith of its development. Many engineers felt that from this point on the airplane's continued modifications produced diminishing returns, that engineering and production efforts in an entirely new airplane would have yielded better results.

The Focke-Wulf FW-190A, sturdier in construction, more manoeuverable at low and medium altitudes, more heavily armed with four cannon and two guns, equipped with wide-track gear that made ground handling much easier and safer, was touted as but one example why the Me-109 should be phased out of production and as quickly as possible be replaced with a superior design.

The Me-109 had, after all, been created in 1934 and there was just so much that could be done to a single design. The time was past due for a replacement.

The German government would have liked nothing better than to build a wholly new airplane, a better fighter than the Me-109G. They would have liked nothing better than (1) to accelerate production of the FW-190, a later design than the Me-109, and (2) convert the Me-109 production lines into whatever machine would be its replacement; but certain practical considerations made a changeover unlikely.

The Me-109 had served as the *only* Luftwaffe fighter until the advent of the Focke-Wulf 190 – and already it had been discovered that above 20,000 feet the performance of the FW-190 deteriorated rapidly. At low and medium altitudes the FW-190 was a superb aircraft and were fighting restricted to such altitudes most pilots would have preferred the machine – but unfortunately, combat was *not* restricted to these heights and was, in fact, taking place more and more often at much higher altitudes. Even the heavy bombers were operating at heights of 20,000 to 26,000 ft, and it was therefore essential to produce a fighter which could attack the bombers and attend to the American fighter escort, which was becoming ever more troublesome as the fighters extended their range. Above 25,000 ft no German pilot exhibited great enthusiasm for fighting Thunderbolts and Mustangs from the cockpit of the FW-190, and the reason was simple enough – in speed, climb and handling the American machines were superior.

So the FW-190, plagued with engine problems and technical difficulties which limited mass production, failed to meet the needs of Germany insofar as a fighter aircraft was concerned, under all the conditions that had to be met.

By sheer elimination, only the Me-109 was left, however outmoded its basic design might be.

Herein, therefore, lay a host of problems – all of which seemed to defy that immediate solution which Germany so desperately needed. With the FW-190 unsatisfactory at high altitudes, the only fighter Germany had for combat at all heights was the improvement to the 109F – the 109G. Were Messerschmitt to create a wholly new machine, and assuming initial prototype testing could be rushed to its completion with a minimum of delay, the time required before full production could begin would be at least one year.

But Germany didn't have the year. Unquestionably there had been a failure much earlier in time, when Germany should have prepared for mass production of the Me-109's successor; but such preparation had not been made and now the time in which to do so no longer existed. (The same problem faced the Japanese. The Zero fighter which fought before World War II in China, and which devastated Allied airpower after the attack on Pearl Harbor, was unquestionably the finest fighter aircraft in the Pacific in 1941. But by 1942, when the Zero's development had reached a dead-end, the Japanese could not afford a massive interruption of production and were forced – as were the Germans with the 109 – to concentrate instead on improving the Zero, and continuing – even accelerating – its production.)

The key to increased performance in a machine such as the Me-109 could be found only in more and more power, and inevitably Messerschmitt was forced along this line. Aside from minor changes and modifications, the Gustav differed from its 109F predecessor through use of the DB-605A-1 engine, which produced 1,475 horsepower compared to the 1,300 horsepower of the late-model 109F series fighters. The power was to increase further through drastic modifications to the engine and every attempt was made continually to achieve ever higher power from the DB engines.

Power meant speed, altitude, and better fighting capability; but with such blessings came liabilities in profusion. The essence of the matter was that an entirely new airplane was needed to utilize best the increased power of the engine. A new design would have resulted in something along the lines of the P-51 Mustang which, with essentially the same power as its 109G competitor, was in almost every respect both a better airplane and a superior fighter.

But time was against the designers of the Me-109G.

The vexing problems of trying to squeeze more out of the 109G than could be obtained through raw engine power led to heated exchanges between German officials and Willy Messerschmitt. In a meeting with Messerschmitt the head of the Technical Office of the Luftwaffe pointed out that while the speed of the Me-109 was perfectly within requirement, what the Luftwaffe needed was a fighter 'with the same speed plus greater range and a better rate of climb'.

Willy Messerschmitt, it has been reported reliably, reacted with a flash of temper. 'What do you want?' he is said to have shouted, 'A fast fighter or a barn door?'

The inference was plain. You could build either a lithe, swift attack fighter or you could build a clumsy machine with long range; but you could not build both. On that point Messerschmitt was emphatic. The German official deferred to Messerschmitt's knowledge.

His response, one might say, was two years in the making, for it was two years later when these same two individuals were forced to run for shelter in Augsburg, which had come under attack by a swarm of Thunderbolt fighters of the Eighth Fighter Command. At the sight of the powerful fighters strafing deep within enemy territory, the official of the Technical Office turned to Willy Messerschmitt with the acid reply:

'Well, there are your barn doors!'

Time obscures whether or not there was a retort on the part of Willy Messerschmitt. But one thing was certain; what he had said was impossible was right there before his eyes – and rather murderously into the bargain.

By May of 1942 the first Me-109G fighters – the Gustav – were rolling off the production lines of several factories. In the late summer of 1942 the airplane was in operational service testing and before the year was out the G models were being flown on the major combat fronts of Germany. It was not yet realized that the future of this airplane would follow a course drastically different from the role played by its predecessors, for until now the Me-109 fighter, except during local theater reverses, had been an airplane carrying out the attack.

But Germany was on the brink of a massive invasion by as many as forty to sixty thousand men every day – the American and British airmen striking at the heart of Nazi power. The great bomber fleets were taking form. Not simply one to two hundred heavy bombers, but four and six hundred and a thousand, and finally as many as 2,500 heavy bombers covered by 1,500 fighters striking from England – in addition to raids from Italy and other Allied fronts surrounding Germany. To the Me-109G would fall the greatest portion of the burden of defense against these prodigious air assaults. The fighter that had been intended to escort German bombers was now defending Germany against enemy bombers.

As noted, the most drastic ultimate change from the F to the G series was the increased power of the Gustav's engines, but several F models served as flying testbeds for the G, which at first featured only minor modifications for the new production model.

The first pre-production batch of twelve Me-109G-0 fighters differed little from their predecessors, since the DB-605A engine was not yet available; the 109G-0 aircraft were fitted with the DB-601E engine of 1,300 horsepower. But when the DB-605A did become available, it featured many modifications; not only did it give more powerful boost (1,475 hp) at take-off, but it produced 1,355 hp at 18,700 ft.

Other major innovations in the G-1 production aircraft included a strengthening of the aircraft structure, and the fitting of a pressurized cabin – an improvement in response to the increasing heights of combat, an arena for which the Me-109G was eminently suited, and where the FW-190, despite many superior qualities, had proved inadequate. Armament comprised one 20-mm MG 151 cannon firing through the propeller hub and two engine-mounted MG 17 guns of 7·9-mm (approximately ·30 caliber).

Immediately production started, demands were made for the powerful Gustav fighters in Africa, and Messerschmitt rushed through the Me-109G-1/Trop for desert combat. To increase firepower in the G-1/Trop the 7·9-mm guns were replaced by 13-mm MG 131 machine guns (slightly larger than the ·50 caliber machine gun of the P-38, P-47 and P-51 and to accommodate the larger MG 131 weapons large fairings over the breech blocks were installed, giving the cowling a characteristic 'bump' which produced the nickname of *Beule*, or *Bump*, for this subvariant.

The subvariants and special modifications came quickly. The G-2 was built without the pressurized cabin of the G-0 and G-1 models, and was designed for the mission of fighter reconnaissance. The Reconnaissance Department at Guyancourt in France built a special gun pack which was mounted to the belly of a G-2 fighter, the guns firing to the *rear* of the airplane. But mounting and aiming problems were so great the test service group abandoned the project.

The additional power of the DB-605A engine was put to good use in the Me-109G-2/R1 fighter bomber version.

Top: **Abandoned Me-109G-1/Trop of JG 27 in North Africa in 1943.** *Bottom:* **The Me-109G-2 reconnaissance fighter**

Me-109G-3 being run up before flight

Two jettisonable fuel tanks were carried beneath the wings, a heavy bomb was shackled beneath the fuselage and to assure clearance of the bomb fins on takeoff engineers jury-rigged one of the oddest takeoff systems of any fighter ever flown – a large 'auxiliary tail wheel' mounted on the fuselage, at a point almost directly beneath the cockpit. After takeoff the pilot pulled a lever in the cockpit to release the wheel, which was lowered to the ground by parachute for re-use.

The 109G-3, except for the new FuG 16 Z radio (replacing the FuG 7A), was identical to the 109G-1, including the pressure cabin. The G-4, which followed in quick order, was itself identical to the G-3, but without the pressurized cabin.

With the 109G-5 the airplane reached another plateau in performance. The new DB-605D engine, with a more powerful super-charger and a methanol/ water injection system (carried in a tank beneath the fuselage and operated by a control in the cockpit) mixing with 100 octane fuel, boosted output to 1,800 hp. This brought emergency-power speeds to above 400 mph and raised the combat ceiling of the airplane to nearly 42,000 feet. No sooner had the 109G-5 gone into service when it was further modified into the Me-109G-5/Rs subvariant. Messerschmitt engineers had continued their attempts to reduce the tendency of the airplane to swing on takeoff and the 109G-5/R2 was their answer. The airplane received a longer tailwheel assembly and a raised vertical fin and rudder; the structural members of the latter were made of wood in the wartime economy of saving the lightweight metals needed for aircraft production. This produced its own minor problem, since the wood construction was heavier than the duralanium normally used in the tail. To compensate for the unexpected weight in the tail a counterweight was bolted beneath the oil tank bracket. The armament of the G-5 series was standardized at the two 13-mm nose guns and the high-velocity 20-mm

MG 151 cannon.

Of all the fighters in the 109 series, the Me-109G-6, in its different variants and forms was manufactured in the greatest number. The 109G-6 was to the latter years of the war, in its use against United States air power, what the 109E models were to the Battle of Britain. It was the airplane that bore the brunt of the most furious air fighting of the war – against the mass formations of heavy bombers and their swift escort fighters.

The G-6 series fighters were powered with different models of the DB-605 engine – the DB-605AM, AS, ASB, ASD or ASM that started at 1,435 and reached 1,800 hp for combat operations. The original G-6 models that entered operational service were intended for bomber intercept missions. The airplane mounted in the nose the two 13-mm guns and a new MK-108 cannon of 30-mm; this latter weapon had a muzzle velocity of only 1,760 feet per minute, but its range and powerful explosive charge made it especially effective against large airplanes such as the B-17 and B-24. In addition to the nose weapons the G-6 variant was fitted out with underwing gondolas, in each a 20-mm MG 151 cannon for a total armament of three cannon and two guns. This was similar to the armament fitted to models earlier than the G-6 variant, but heavier guns with faster firing rates made the ordnance of the G-6 far deadlier than ever before. The need for such firepower was so critical that the Me-109G-6/U4 was equipped with *three* 30-mm cannon and two 13-mm nose guns, a combination that had a telling effect against the American raiders.

At the same time the heavy armament posed its own problems. The heavier weight of the airplane, which sometimes carried a belly tank for additional fuel, necessitated beefing up the landing gear. The empty weight of the airplane was in the area of 6,000 lbs (specific weights depended upon mission flown) and the loaded weight was exceeding 8,000 lbs. Without strengthening, losses from 'wiping out' the gear would have become critical.

The other problem plaguing the ME-109G series, especially such types as

Me-109G-5 with its jettisonable
methanol/water booster tank

The most important variant of the G series, the Me-109G-6, with its underwing cannon in twin gondolas

Me-109G-6
Engine: Daimler-Benz 605A-1, 1,475 hp.
Armament: 2 x 13.1-mm machine guns
and 3 x 20-mm cannon. *Speed:* 387 mph
at 22,970 ft. *Ceiling:* 39,750 ft. *Range:*
615 miles. *Weights:* 5,900 lbs empty and
6,970 lbs loaded. *Span:* 36 ft 6½ ins.
Length: 29 ft 8 ins

the G-6/U4 variants with their heavy firepower, had to do with the fluid nature of the air war. The heavy ordnance was required for attacking bombers, but the fighters also had to defend themselves against American escort fighters. The dilemma was that without the additional cannon the German fighters lost their effectiveness against the bombers. With the cannon the Me-109G suffered so severely in performance that it became easy prey for the American escorts. Many of the G-series fighters, equipped with the heavy ordnance, had to have these units removed – somewhat frustrating to the pilots involved.

Referring to the Me-109F and G models with the gondolas beneath the wings, Galland was led to comment that the machine 'defaced in this way was as good as useless for fighter combat . . . when the fighter escort of the Americans became more and more effective, the "bathtubs" had to be removed again. The escorting fighters became the primary target. Shooting down bombers took second place.'

Galland refers to the FW-190 as much more suitable for such engagements. Everyone in the defense units protecting Germany, it seemed, 'clamoured for FW-190s.' Yet massive production of the FW-190 would not have swung the balance for, as Galland also noted: 'One of its weaknesses was that above 21,000 feet its performance fell off rapidly. As the B-17 usually came in at that height, it was of course handicapped in combating the American fighter escort.'

The only solution appeared to be that of stripping the weight and drag from the Me-109G fighters so that they could tackle the American fighters while the FW-190s went after the bombers – a strange parallel to the Battle of Britain where the Spitfires tried to assure that the Hurricanes

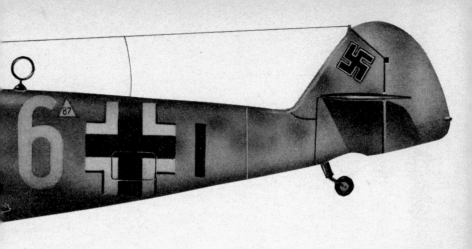

could last through German fighter attacks in order to get at the German bombers!

To build up night-fighter units, the G-6 was further modified into the 109G-6/U4N subvariant equipped with warning and homing receivers with a maximum range of about thirty miles. The *Naxos Z* radar units (the antenna was housed behind the cockpit; the signal received by the pilot indicated to him the direction but not the distance of his target) installed in Me-109G-6/UFN and FW-190A-5/U2N gave this group a burst of success in 'wild boar' night-fighting tactics against British bombers. The success waned when less-experienced pilots making night landings in the heavily loaded fighters ran up an alarming number of crashes.

These night-landing losses brought up a sore point with many critics of the Me-109G. There was no question but that the heavy overloads imposed upon the airplane, increasing still further its already high wing loading, had forced a deterioration in the handling and control characteristics

of the machine. There are some historians who feel the criticism at its worst was fully justified. William Green, for example, states that the 109G fighters 'could not be flown in a landing circuit with flaps and undercarriage down other than at full throttle, and experienced German operational pilots have described its landing characteristics as 'vicious'.'

Perhaps this was a matter of view – or of trying to retain the objective viewpoint. In their study of the Me-109G, J R Smith and I Primmer noted that despite the definite lowering of handling qualities under certain conditions of the fighter, 'it is the opinion of many ex-Gustav pilots that it is gross exaggeration to call the aircraft a 'killer.' Such published claims as those which state that the late variants could only be flown in the landing regime at full throttle were dismissed by ex-Messerschmitt test pilot Karl Baur as utterly absurd.'

The fighter-bomber variant in the G-6 series was the 109G-6/R1 which could carry a bomb of 1,100 pounds; the heaviest bomb load of any 109

This Me-109G-6/R2 Trop of JG 3 in the south of Russia is equipped with twin WGr 21 infantry type rockets for ground support or for attacks on American bomber streams

For operational training, numbers of G-1 aircraft were modified to a tandem cockpit configuration with the instructor in the rear one

variant-in the series. The next model in the ground-attack fighter-support modifications, the 109G-6/R2, eliminated the underwing gondolas in favor of a WG 21 rocket-launching tube beneath each wing. Few pilots took well to the rocket tubes which disturbed the airstream so severely that control during approach and landing became something of a small adventure. Events proved the installation more troublesome than was warranted by its limited success and the 109G-6/R2 models were reconverted in the field back to their underwing cannon armament. The 109G-6/R2 Trop was identical to the G-6/R2 except for the installation of tropical dust filters for the engine and the use of the pilot survival pack. A number of 109G-6/R2 fighter-bombers, in company with FW-190A-6/R2 aircraft, carried out a series of sharp and effective raids against Allied invasion shipping off Sicily; this was, however, one of the rare examples of the airplanes' success in this role.

The Me-109G-7 never reached the production line. Messerschmitt proposed this airplane to incorporate all the changes and modifications already impressed into the many G variants. At the last moment, before commitment to production, the G-7 version was abandoned for the projected G-10 model.

Fast reconnaissance became the mission for the 109G-8, which in production was fitted with the early tail assembly, was built with only the two nose guns for armament, was equipped with special cameras, and came into service in late 1943.

The 109G-9, like the G-7, was a paper project abandoned before production tooling was committed.

Fastest of the 109G series was the G-10 which, powered with the DB-605D engine with power boost, reached a maximum speed of 428 mph at 24,250 ft. But more important than this high speed was its capability as an interceptor from a standing start, the 109G-10 under full power could reach 20,000 ft in six minutes. The range was considerably less than in even the older E models, but the figure of 350 miles was the penalty paid for speed and climb performance, and could always be augmented with a jettisonable tank. This proved to be necessary since under the best of conditions the 109G-10 had an endurance of less than one hour, woefully inadequate for takeoff and climb, vectoring, positioning for attack, carrying out firing passes, and returning to base.

Shortly after entering service the G-10 was tested as the Me-109G-10/U4 with two 30-mm cannon in a pack mounted beneath the belly, and this armament was critical to the airplane's mission as the normal ordnance consisted only of the two 13-mm nose guns, with the engine-

mounted 30-mm cannon considered an optional fitting! Galland must have felt dismay when the G-10 appeared with no more firepower than the first Me-109 fighters assigned to the Luftwaffe, and rather quickly the 'optional assignment' of the engine cannon was changed to standard armament, while to rectify the airplane's inadequate firepower as a bomber destroyer, the belly pack of two cannon was fitted. Unfortunately for those pilots engaged in bomber interception, the belly pack was cursed with technical problems and was soon abandoned, to be replaced with a long-range tank which could *not* be jettisoned. This was another of those inexplicable 'retrogressive' steps as, with the belly tank in place, the 109G was outflown and outfought by the American escort fighters.

Next to make its appearance was the Me-109G-10/R2 which was built with the new wooden tail, the lengthened tailwheel installation and, to meet a long-existing visibility problem, was equipped with the 'Galland Hood,' a streamlined cockpit canopy that increased measurably the pilot's visibility. Immediately after the G-10/R2 appeared the G-10/R6 went into service, its distinction being the FuG 25a electronic equipment for 'friend-or-foe' identification.

The Me-109G-12 appeared at training bases. This was a standard Me-109G-1 airframe modified as a two-seat trainer, tandem seating, and with a bulged rear canopy to improve visibility for the instructor, some models retaining the two nose machine guns for firing practice. In the final desperate months of the war many G-12 trainers were hastily fitted out with additional armament and thrown into combat.

The Me-109G-11, G-13 and G-15 designations were assigned to proposed subvariants that failed to reach the 'hardware' stage.

The end of the line for operational 109G fighters was the Me-109G-14, a basic 109G-6 with the new Galland Hood, and which was powered with different variants of the DB-605 engine. The G-14 was loaded down with heavy armament for its mission as a ground-support aircraft; the machine was fitted with the two 13-mm nose guns, a 20-mm MG 151 cannon firing through the propeller hub, and two 20-mm cannon beneath the wings. The need for increased firepower was so great that many G-14s were overloaded with additional 20-mm cannon beneath the wings to make a total armament of five 20-mm cannon and the two 13-mm guns. In addition to this formidable firepower the airplane carried a heavy bomb in a fuselage rack. Many G-14s, instead of the extra wing cannon, had a final armament of the two mg's, three cannon, fuselage bomb of 550 pounds, *and* two rocket-launching tubes beneath the wings. The G-14/Trop was assigned to desert areas; the G-14r/2 was a hasty change that used the wooden tail of greater height but kept the shorter tailwheel leg.

Me-109G-10
Engine: Daimler-Benz 605D + MW50 boost. *Armament:* 2 x 13.1-mm machine guns and 1 x 30-mm cannon. *Speed:* 428 mph at 25,000 ft. *Ceiling:* 41,400 ft. *Range:* 350 miles. *Weight:* 8,115 lbs loaded. *Span:* 32 ft 6½ ins. *Length:* 29 ft 8 ins

The final Gustav to roll off the production line was the G-16. The airplane, which featured the old-style cockpit canopy, was fitted with heavy armor plating as protection in ground-attack missions. Some G-16 models, according to Nowarra, were equipped with the Naxos radar units, but as it happened, the G-16 failed to reach operational service.

Production of the Me-109G fighters in 1943 came to 6,418 machines. In 1944 the figure rose to a startling 14,212 aircraft, including the G models and successor designs. During the several months of 1945 that the factories were able to continue production 2,969 Me-109 fighters were delivered. Many of these failed to see active service, being destroyed either on the pro-

duction flight lines, during delivery, or on the ground after delivery to their operational units.

During 1943 despite its critical needs for the airplane, Germany exported one hundred and forty five Me-109Gs to Bulgaria, seventy to Finland, two to Japan, seventy to Rumania, fifteen to Slovakia, fifty nine to Hungary, and twenty five to Spain.

During 1943 the Luftwaffe was pressing the need for a high-altitude modification of the Me-109F for special missions. The first variants flown, the Me-109H-0, were rebuilt F models and retained the older DB-601E engine until the more powerful DB-605A with power boost could be supplied. Engineers increased by six and a half feet the wingspan, and installed a new tailplane; the latter also had a greater span and was reinforced with external struts, as in the 109E.

Despite the need for light weight the 109H retained a nose armament of two 13-mm guns and one 30-mm cannon. The operational ceiling for

the reconnaissance fighter was an impressive 47,000 to 50,000 ft, depending upon weight and atmospheric conditions – even at its lower figure the 109H could operate beyond the reach of any opposing operational fighter. The maximum speed was 465 mph, and there was no question but that the Me-109H-1 could both run away from and outclimb anything it might have encountered in the air.

But the new wing and major modifications exacted their penalty. In diving or steep turn manoeuvers the lengthened wing suddenly vibrated or 'fluttered.' The few H-1 variants that went into active service were restricted from deliberately engaging in combat and were assigned to high-altitude reconnaissance missions where they could overfly – or run away from – any interceptors. A series of 109H models was proposed by Messerschmitt with even higher performance, but the wing flutter was so serious a problem that the Luftwaffe cancelled the program and turned instead to the Ta-152H reconnaissance fighter by Focke-Wulf.

The Me-109I was a design proposal that failed to reach any test models before it was cancelled. Spanish versions of the Me-109 received the Me-109J designation by Messerschmitt.

The last 109s to go into production and operational service made up the Me-109K series, which went into operations during 1944. There was little externally to distinguish the G from the K models, for the latter was essentially a G aircraft with structural and other minor improvements. All K models, of which there were fourteen subvariants, were built with the Galland Hood. Only four of the subvariants, however, the 109K-2, K-4, K-6 and K-14, went into full production.

As in the development of previous models, the initial groups of 109K-0 aircraft were standard G airframes, powered with the boosted DB-605D engine. There was little change with the K-2 and K-4 subvariants. They were powered with either the DB-605ASCM or the DB-605ADCM engine; the only basic difference between the

Top: Very heavily armed, the
Me-109G-14 featured the 'Galland'
hood for better visibility, and was the
last G variant to see service in the war.
Bottom: The Me-109K series was an
improved version of the G series with
more powerful engines. The K-4,
shown here, had a pressurised cockpit

two fighters was that the K-4 was
built with a pressurized cabin.
Standard armament included two
15-mm MG 151 weapons over the engine
and an engine mounted MK 103 or 108
cannon. The engine fitted to the K4
delivered 1,500 hp normally and could
be boosted to 2,000 hp. At 20,000 ft the
109K-4 had a top speed of 452 mph, and
it climbed swiftly to its service ceiling
of 41,000 ft. In every flight respect it
was an outstanding aircraft. From
start of takeoff roll to 16,400 ft required
less than seven minutes. The maximum weight was 7,400 lbs. Range at a

weight of 6,834 lbs was 356 miles.

The K-6 version was more heavily
armed. Two 13-mm guns were mounted
atop the engine, the nose cannon was
of 30-mm, and another two 30-mm
cannon were carried beneath the
wings. The gross weight of this fighter
rose to 7,920 lbs. At its best operating
height of 19,700 ft the 109K-6 had a top
speed of 440 mph.

The production story of the Me-109
ended with the Me-109K-14, of which
only two aircraft saw combat action.
The DB-605L with power boost gave a
top speed of 455 mph, and the lessened
armament of two machine guns and
one 30-mm cannon in the nose
testified to the critical need of the
Luftwaffe fighters to defend themselves against the Thunderbolts and
Mustangs.

But it was too late. The two 109K-14
fighters that went into combat with
JG 52 were simply the final act in the
destruction of Germany.

The German aces

In most works written on the Me-109 and the FW-190 fighters there appears an inescapable judgement that both these machines were of such vintage they should have been replaced well before 1945. Nowarra, for example, states that both 'the Me-109 and FW-190 were obsolete . . . ' This is difficult to understand, because on this basis just about every fighter aircraft of World War II was obsolete. For example, with the exception of the Grumman F6F Hellcat series, every American fighter plane flown in combat during World War II was either built or had been designed prior to the war – in this instance the date of war being December 7, 1941. The primary American fighter aircraft – Lockheed P-38 Lightning, Bell P-39 Airacobra, Curtiss P-40, Republic P-47 Thunderbolt, North American P-51 Mustang, Northrop P-61 Black Widow, Grumman F4F Wildcat, Grumman F7F Tigercat, Chance-Vought F4U Corsair – all were of prewar design or manufacture.

A revealing comparison of the Me-109 and the P-47 can be obtained by viewing the German fighter as it was seen through the eyes of one of the United States' best fighter aces of World War II – Robert S. Johnson. Major Johnson, who flew the P-47 in combat for a period of eleven months, scored twenty eight aerial victories. But there is greater significance in his achievement when we realize that his combat was all against the best German pilots on the western front, that he fought the best of the Me-109 and FW-190 line, that all his kills were in the air, and that all his kills were German fighters. The finest accolade to be paid Major Johnson is that his opponents consider him to be one of the outstanding fighter pilots of World War II.

In reviewing this initial encounter with the Me-109, the reader is advised to recall the ability of the Me-109 pilot to escape British fighters by throwing the 109 into a steep dive, which invariably enabled the German fighter swiftly to elude its pursuer. That advantage, as will be shown, vanished with the advent of the Thunderbolt, as Major Johnson relates:

'Two days later we flew a Ramrod to Gilze Rijen, and again I flew wing position for Jerry Johnson. We were just inland, nearing Woensdrecht, when I called, "Four bandits, three o'clock high, going one-eight-zero degrees to us. This is Keyworth White 2, Out." Jerry snapped back, "Roger." The enemy planes came around in a wide, sweeping turn, sliding onto our tails for a stern attack. "Let's go!" White Flight lifted up, turned to rush directly into the Germans. Immediately the Messerschmitts rolled in a shallow dive, then jerked up in steep zoom climbs. I hung back, covering Jerry as he raced after the enemy leader. In a flash a second fighter whirled around, streaking after Jerry.'

[1] *THUNDERBOLT!*, by Robert S. Johnson with Martin Caidin (Rinehart & Company, Inc.: New York.)

'. . . and then as I turned more closely I gained on him . . .' – the inevitable post-mortem on a kill

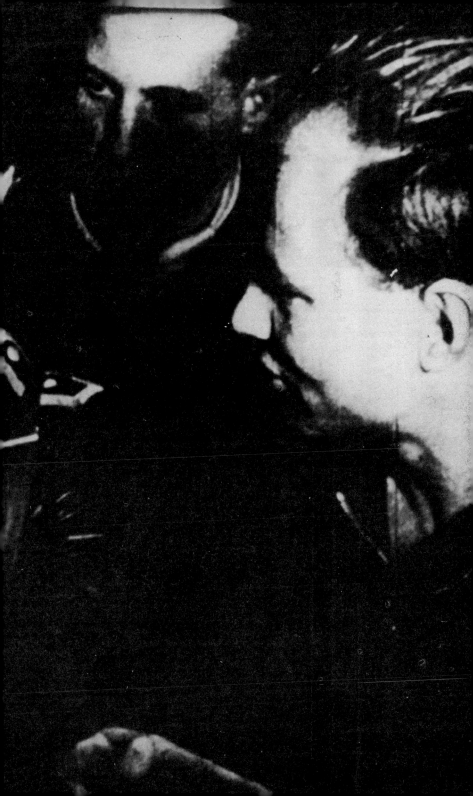

'I hit the throttle, giving the P-47 her head. The moment the second Me-109 spotted me coming in, he snapped over in a sharp turn and fled to the north. Jerry was only 90 degrees to him as I swung on to his tail. I closed in rapidly to one hundred and fifty yards, prepared to fire. Suddenly Jerry kicked rudder and sent a burst into the Me-109. A good boy in that Messerschmitt; he pulled into a terrific turn, kicked his plane into a spin. I rolled and dove, waiting for the Me-109 to make his first full turn. I knew just where he'd be for his second turn, and I opened fire at this spot.'

'Sure enough! The Messerschmitt spun right into my stream of bullets. Immediately he kicked out of the spin and dove vertically. Oh no, you don't! I rolled the Jug, and from 27,000 feet raced after the fleeing Me-109. The Messerschmitt seemed to crawl as the Thunderbolt fell out of the sky. I lined up directly behind the sleek fighter, squeezed the trigger. Eight heavy guns converged their fire.'

'My second kill vanished in a blinding explosion that tore the fighter into shreds . . . '

As a 'present' with which to start off 1944, engineers installed new propellers on the Thunderbolts flown by the 56th Fighter Group, to which Bob Johnson belonged. Johnson reported that our 'engineering officers were making a terrific fuss over a new propeller designed specifically for the Thunderbolt. They insisted that the fat paddle blades of the new propellers would bring a tremendous boost in performance . . . We listened to their enthusiastic ramblings with a grain of salt – and never were we more mistaken.'

Johnson relates that on a test flight at 8,000 ft 'I pulled the Thunderbolt into a steep climb. Normally she'd zoom quickly and then slow down, rapidly approaching a stall. But now – the Jug soared up like she'd gone crazy. Another Thunderbolt was in the air, and I pulled alongside, signalling for a climb. I'm not an engineering officer, and I don't know the exact ft

Smoke beginning to trail from its fuselage, an Me-109G goes down after being hit by the fire from an American escort fighter over Germany

per minute that we climbed. But I left that other fighter behind as if he were standing still. The Jug stood on her tail and howled her way into the sky. Never again did a FW-190 or an Me-109 outclimb me in the Thunderbolt. The new prop was worth 1,000 horsepower more, and then some. Later I had the opportunity to mix it up with a Spitfire 9B . . . I was astonished as we both poured the coal to our fighters, and the Thunderbolt just ran away from the Spit.'

The effectiveness of the new propeller is told by Johnson on a mission shortly afterward. The year is 1944 –

'On 6th January I met one of the Luftwaffe old-timers, one of the toughest pilots I've ever fought. Near Coblenz the Group raced in a dive after fifteen Focke-Wulfs. Gabreski locked onto a Kraut's tail and the German wingman came hard after Gabby. I saw him swinging in, turned hard, and made a head-on pass. The Focke-Wulf jerked up steeply to the right, turning away. I threw the Jug into a roll and went after him. He put his fighter into a wicked turn, but I kept rolling and firing, sticking like glue to his tail. He steepened the climb, but with the new propeller the Thunderbolt never let go. I kept rolling, squeezing out bursts, scoring hits steadily. He turned, twisting violently to lose me.'

'I stayed with him following every move, still firing, still scoring. Abruptly he flicked over and dove, jerking from side to side to avoid my fire. He was terrific, one of the very best. *But the dive was his mistake. Again and again the Germans tried to break out of a tough position by diving. Never did they learn!* [Italics Added] The moment my nose went down the engine and propeller wound up in a scream and narrowed the gap. I went in close, less than fifty yards, and squeezed out a long burst. The bullets tore into his cockpit and left wing root, flaming a fuel tank. The Focke-Wulf tumbled crazily, end over end, and tore apart. Number Eleven . . .'

Johnson relates a combat with an Me-109 –

'A mile above me a B-17 swooped out of control, flames streaming from the engines and the crew leaping into space. Two Me-109s circled the falling giant, snapping out machine-gun fire at the men helpless in their parachutes. The Krauts had their fighters wide open, black smoke pouring from their exhausts. I slammed the throttle forward and climbed, the paddle blades hauling me up quickly. The leader of the two German fighters raced straight ahead for safety while his wingman broke to the right. By now I was raging with anger; I was determined to get at least one of the two planes. The lead Messerschmitt suddenly stopped smoking. It was a complete giveaway; I knew that at this instant he'd cut power. I chopped the throttle to prevent overrunning the enemy fighter. I skidded up to my right, half rolled to my left, wings vertical. He turned sharply to the left; perfect! Now – stick hard back, rudder pedals coordinating smoothly. The Thunderbolt whirled around, slicing inside the Messerschmitt. I saw the pilot look up behind him, gaping, as the Thunderbolt loomed inside of his turn, both wings flaming with all eight guns.'

'This boy had never seen a Thunderbolt really roll; he was convinced I'd turned inside him. At once the Me-109 straightened out and dove. They never learned! Now I had him dead to rights; I closed rapidly as the ground rushed toward our two planes, squeezing out short bursts. White flashes leaped all over the fuselage and wings. I was scoring; good hits that were cutting up the Messerschmitt. He didn't give up easily, and racked his fighter around in a wicked left turn. I got another burst into him; some of the slugs tore into his canopy. The fighter belched forth a thick cloud of smoke and seemed almost to stop in the air; then I was overshooting him. I jerked back on the stick, flashing over the smoking airplane. I saw only a flaming mess on the ground.'

'Two Thunderbolts closed on my own fighter; Sam Hamilton and Joe Perry. "Hey Sam," I called, "is that him there on the ground?" Sam chuckled. "Hell, yes, that's him." And *that* made me feel better.'

As much a part of the Me-109 story as the airplane in combat is the record of the German pilots who became the top-scoring aces of World War II. Every top German ace at one

time or another flew the Me-109 and some aces, such as Hans J Marseille (credited with 158 kills before his own death), flew only the Me-109 in its different variants. Following is a list of German aces who are each credited with more than 150 kills –

Erich Hartmann	352
Gerhard Barkhorn	301
Guenther Rall	275
Otto Kittel	267
Walter Nowotny	258
Wilhelm Batz	242
Theo Weissenberger	238
Erich Rudorffer	222
Heinrich Bar	220
Heinz Ehrler	220
Hans Philipp	213
Walter Schuck	206
Anton Hafner	204
Helmut Lippert	203
Hermann Graf	202
Walter Krupinski	197
Anton Hackl	190
Joachim Brendle	189
Max Stotz	189
Joachim Kirschner	185
Werner Brandle	180
Gunther Josten	178
Joh. Steinhoff	176
Gunther Schack	174
Heinz Schmidt	173
Emil Lang	173
E W Reinert	169
Horst Adameit	166
Wolf D Wilcke	161
Gordon Gollob	160
Hans J Marseille	158
Gerhard Thyben	157
Hans Beisswenger	152
Peter Duttmann	152

All this leads to some rather interesting and remarkable statistics.

The Germans list thirty four aces as having scored 150 or more kills in air-to air combat.

Those thirty four men, according to the official German figures, shot down in aerial combat no less than 6,902 enemy aircraft.

There were another sixty aces who the Germans state shot down between 100 and 150 aircraft each. Those sixty men accounted for another 7,095 machines.

Thus, according to the official German records, ninety four aces of the Luftwaffe accounted for 13,997 enemy machines shot down in aerial combat.

Major Erich Hartmann, 352 kills, the Ace of Aces of the Second World War, served on the Eastern Front where he was known as the 'Black Devil'. His career started in 1942

Major Gerhard Barkhorn, 301 kills, served in the East and the West, scoring only in the East. He always insisted on using the Me-109

Major Günther Rall, 275 kills, flew in the same unit as Barkhorn, JG 52, on the Eastern Front, and like Hartmann and Barkhorn survived the war

Lieutenant-Colonel Heinrich Bär, 220 kills, started as a sergeant and scored his first kill in September 1939. He was the highest scorer against the RAF and USAAF in Europe with 124 of his kills in this theatre

Nearly fourteen thousand planes shot down by less than one hundred men . . .

Such statistics make one stop and think – especially when these staggering claims are contrasted with the records of the United States' top aces: Bong (40), McGuire (38), McCampbell (34), and Gabreski (31), Britain's top ace, Johnny Johnson, had but 38 kills. Yet the German Steinhoff with 'only' 176 confirmed air kills was 'only' the 20th ranking ace of Germany.

The Luftwaffe statisticians make much of the fact that most of these kills were registered on the Russian front. In fact, Erich Rudorffer on 6th November 1943 is credited with thirteen kills in a single battle engagement that lasted seventeen minutes. This is by no means an impossibility since on 24th October 1944, Dave McCampbell in a Hellcat shot down nine confirmed (plus two probables) when he roared into a flight of Japanese single-engine bombers obviously flown by green pilots who 'just sat there' while he flew, aimed, and fired to his heart's content.

Another point to consider is that the German pilots sometimes flew from two to five or even more sorties in a single day, their home fields being 'only a stone's throw' from the combat area. They flew almost constantly. Even the sceptics admit that some of the veteran Luftwaffe pilots flew from 1,000 to 2,000 missions during their combat years – and a seasoned veteran with a superior airplane has a lot going for him under these conditions.

Equally important is that in the latter years of the war the Germans didn't go to the enemy   the enemy went after them. That meant that German pilots who were shot down often lived to fight another day, for they crash-landed or bailed out over their own territory. Barkhorn, who claims 301 kills on the Russian front, was shot down at least sixteen times. Nowotny, who claims 255 victories, was shot down right after his first kill. He managed to avoid this nasty experience again until just before the end of the war when he was shot down for a second time in his Me-262 jet fighter.

But can the extraordinary kills which are claimed for Germany's fighter aces be accepted?

Lt. General E R Quesada, USAF, who wrote a brief introduction to Heinz Knoke's book on life as a Luftwaffe fighter pilot, is doubtful:

'Some details of this volume seem exaggerated to me. (Our own pilots could also, on occasion, do some fancy fact-stretching.) For example, I do not believe, as Knoke does, that any German ace shot down one hundred and fifty Allied planes. Here and there his book contains other statements which I regard as obvious Nazi propaganda, swallowed whole by an eager youth.'

Wing Commander Asher Lee remarked –

'Such men as Moelders, Wick and Marseille were certainly first-class pilots, equal in caliber to any of their opposite numbers in the Allied Air forces; but their mammoth claims of air combat victories, running sometimes over the two hundred mark, were absurdly exaggerated. Nevertheless this glorification of the stars often served to urge on other young German fighter pilots. At the same time it was sometimes so transparent that it acted as a boomerang. On one occasion a young German ace who shall be nameless (except that he was one of the three stars mentioned above) returned from an engagement with Spitfires over the English Channel and claimed three of the Spitfires shot down. The ground staff noted that his guns had not fired and that all his ammunition was intact in the aircraft. The story was circulated amongst the squadron and was transmitted to other flying units. The score of the ace pilot rose, but his stock fell, and he soon acquired a German staff appointment!'

Roland P Beamont, whom we have met earlier in these pages, noted –

' . . . the individual scores of leading pilots makes interesting but scarcely credible reading. One feels that in accepting German "loss records" as fact the author [referring to Edward Sims] has perhaps rather naively ignored the circumstances under which these records were compiled; namely Hitler's propaganda-ridden Germany.'

'Similarly the lists of British, American and German leading scorers imply that the latter were some form

Major Moelders was one of the Luftwaffe's first great aces in France and on the Eastern Front. His extraordinary career started in Spain

of supermen. Where were these men who could shoot down six of our fighters in one fight and more than a dozen in one day? In thirty-eight months of operation over the Channel and Europe between 1939-1945 and in six hundred and thirty operational hours, one never came across them nor anyone who had. The German fighter pilot seemed no better than ours in 1940, and a lot less good by 1944. One remains unconvinced that differences in methods of recording victories have not given a completely misleading impression of the capabilities of the German leaders.'

And, finally, the comment of the RAF's Group Captain J E 'Johnny' Johnson, the top British ace of World War II with 38 kills:

'I have found it possible to make a detailed check of some of the claims of a well-known German pilot who has been called the "unrivalled virtuoso of the fighter pilots." His greatest day in the Western Desert was on September 1st, 1942 when he claimed seventeen victories, eight of them in the space of ten minutes. But our own records show that on this day we lost a total of only eleven aeroplanes, including two Hurricanes, a type which the German pilot did not claim. In fact, some of our losses occurred when he was on the ground.'

The rare ones

The constant use of any one airplane, especially when it has been produced in such quantity as the Me-109, invariably transcends its normal or intended role. The Me-109 was designed and built as a fighter, pure and simple. Very quickly after its introduction into operational service it was pressed into use as a ground-support machine, first with its permanent weapons in the form of machine guns and cannon and then, as the war progressed, with bombs and rockets. The events of war often dictate desperate expedients, and the Me-109, intended to combat bombers with its conventional weapons, was finally thrown into battle against American bombers with both rockets and bombs. German pilots on their own initiative experimented with dropping bombs into the midst of large American bomber formations. The attack demanded skill and timing as the bomb would explode after so many seconds of free fall. This required the Me-109 pilot to fly an exact course above the American raiders and to drop his weapon at precisely the required height. If he aimed well the bomb would explode within the formations. A direct hit was not required since the blast effect was often enough either to wreck an airplane or send it careening out of control into another.

For a while German Me-109 pilots achieved some success with this method. But its demise was inevitable, once American escort fighters made their appearance. Encumbered by the weight and drag of a bomb, no Me-109 pilot could long survive when attacked by escort fighter pilots all too eager to mix it up with the enemy.

The Me-109 (as well as the FW-190) played another and even more bizarre role as an attack aircraft. This involved an Me-109 fighter attached by rigid struts above a Junkers Ju-88 twin-engined bomber; such combinations were known as the *Beethoven* or *Mistel* composite. The plan called for the bomber to be unmanned and filled with approximately four tons of high explosives, sometimes in the form of a hollow charge. Locked together the two planes took off with all three engines operating and the whole affair guided by the Me-109 pilot who, near his objective, dove steeply toward the ground and at a predetermined distance released his fighter from the explosives-packed bomber, which continued on into the target. There is some argument as to how this project got under way, but the idea of a fighter attached to another machine began with an attempt to create a novel way of transporting gliders. Engineers reasoned that instead of

An Me-109 pick-a-back on a DFS 230 glider in one of the first tests of the 'Mistel' idea feasability

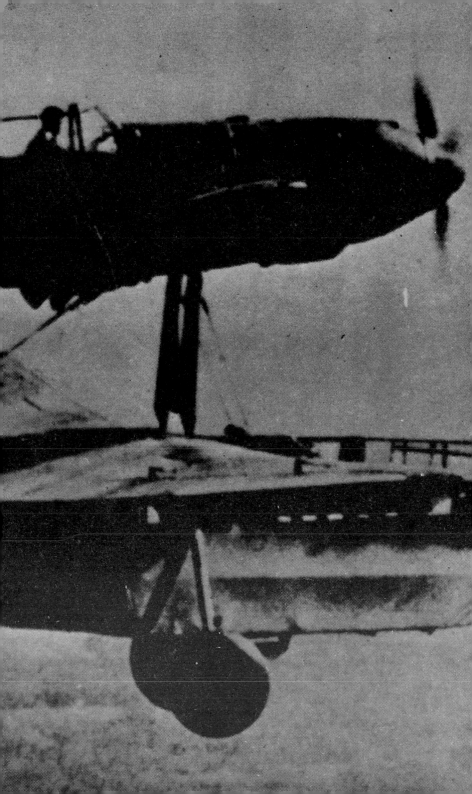

towing a glider it might be possible to create a rigid structure between a powered machine and the glider; near its objective, the glider would be cut free to descend under control of its own pilot. The early tests, carried out under the name of *Starr-Schlepp* – or Rigid Glider Tug – involved low-powered aircraft and the DFS-230 glider, which had to be towed into the air, after which the aircraft engine sufficed to maintain level flight. Later a Me-109E-3 was mounted above the DFS-230, allowing the combined aircraft structure to take off, fly and land under its own power.

The need to deliver heavier explosive loads with accuracy and the success of the Me-109E-3/DFS-230 combination led to the concept of joining the Me-109 with the Ju-88. The first combat composites were made up of Me-109F-4 fighters attached rigidly to Ju-88A-4 bombers carrying 7,700 pounds of explosives. Later, 109G-6 fighters were used with the Ju-88 (and FW-190s were used with the Ju-88G-1). The Me-109/Ju-88 (used in the Normandy invasion) weighed approximately 40,000 pounds and the cruising speed, over a range of about 420 miles, was 280 mph. Upon releasing the bomber the fighter still retained between 450 and 500 miles range capability, since on the way to the target the Me-109 drew fuel from tanks within the Ju-88. Normally the fighter released the bomber at an altitude of 3,000 to 10,000 feet, after which the Ju-88 continued toward the target, depending upon the angle of dive, at between 350 and 400 mph. Far more effort was put into this project than could be justified by results. Most of the Ju-88s prepared for such missions were either destroyed by Allied fighters in strafing attacks or were captured at the close of the war.

Those of us who have followed the career of the Me-109 have always wondered just how this fighter would have held up in fighter-*vs*-fighter combats with the Grumman F6F Hellcat. The latter machine had a much faster rate of climb and was far more manoeuverable. Indeed, the F6F was the only fighter in the Allied camp that, according to testimony of the Japanese pilots themselves, could turn inside the agile Zero. With its speed, climb, heavy firepower, and manoeuv-erability, the Hellcat might have proven a lethal opponent for the Me-109. Unfortunately for enthusiasts, the meeting of Hellcat and Me-109 was known to have taken place only once during World War II, and this was on 8th May 1944, when Hellcats of the carrier H.M.S. *Emperor* flying off Norway encountered a mixed bag of Me-109s and FW-190s. Two Me-109s and one FW-190 were shot down without loss to the attacking Grummans.

Strangely enough, the final combat between British naval fighters and the Me-109 took place between the German fighter and Grumman Wildcats – export versions of the old F4F. Wildcats of 882 Squadron flying over southern Norway ran into a swarm of Me-109s which, according to the British pilots, must have been flown by men who were quite inexperienced. In the swift battle that ensued four Wildcat pilots each shot down an Me-109 without loss to their own number.

We have noted earlier that hundreds of Me-109 variants were either sold or sent to nations outside of Germany, and that many of these were used by Germany's wartime allies against their common enemy, and that, on one occasion at least, German pilots found themselves fighting against Me-109Es that had been sent to Yugoslavia before the two countries became open enemies. One of the stranger sides to the history of the Me-109 belongs to those fighters that were sent to Switzerland, for these aircraft were used on many occasions to attack both German and American fighters and bombers! The Swiss used everything from the Me-109C up through the G model, although the latter, suffering from poor workmanship plaguing the 109 production lines, were grounded so often they saw little service with the Swiss Air Force. The others, however, established a history of brisk fighting with machines that crossed the Swiss borders.

The first open combat took place on 10th May 1940, when a Swiss Me-109E on patrol intercepted a Ju-88 flying in the direction of Basle. Marked with brilliant red-and-white striping, the Swiss 109E fired a burst of tracers across the nose of the Junkers. Immediately the bomber gunners returned the fire. The Swiss pilot swung around in full attack and the Ju-88 shied off, its crew running for nearby clouds to make good their escape. Later that same day another Swiss 109E found itself exchanging deliberate fire with a German bomber. This time the Swiss pilot attacked a Heinkel He-111 near Altenrheim and shot out one engine; the Swiss pilot ceased his firing when the German bomber crossed the border. Other fighters one week later, near Lignieres, pursued another He-111 and when the bomber fired back vigorously, the Me-109Es closed in and shot down the airplane. What had begun as a war of nerves and brief exchanges of gunfire had become a campaign. Swiss 109s were taking off on emergency scrambles as the Germans ignored the legality of Swiss airspace. Under orders to press home their attacks the Swiss pilots, before the month was out, shot down two more He-111 bombers, near Ursins and Lutter.

When the Swiss ignored Goering's bellicose threats of retaliation, the Luftwaffe was ordered to teach the little country a sharp lesson. Starting during the first week of June 1940, formations of He-111 bombers appeared over Switzerland accompanied by strong forces of Me-110 twin-engined fighters. The stage was now set for fierce air battles between German aircraft on both sides – with Swiss 109s against Luftwaffe 110s. If there was any question that the Me-110 was a failure as a long-range *fighter* the Swiss ended the doubts. Two Me-110s and one He-111 went down before the guns of the out-numbered but fiercely fighting Swiss pilots, who lost only one of their own number, an Me-109C (Swiss – J-399). The pilot bailed out but with a parachute ripped by German fire the canopy failed to deploy and he was killed. Swiss reaction was, understandably, rather violent.

Within four days the enraged Germans were back, looking for anything in the air with Swiss markings. Six Me-110s swarmed against a biplane and blew it out of the air. That same day Swiss fighter-control received word that thirty-two Me-110 fighters were orbiting in a wide pattern and at different heights above the Jura Mountains, openly daring the Swiss to come up and fight. The first Swiss aircraft to reach the scene, mainly to confirm the reports of the enemy, found themselves attacked by a diving swarm of Me-110s. Immediately the Swiss pilots dove into nearby clouds, intending to break out on the other side of the clouds and hit the Germans unexpectedly from another quarter. It didn't work; the veteran Me-110 pilots simply turned and set up their trap and as the Swiss 109Es emerged from the clouds they stumbled into a storm of heavy cannon and machine gun fire.

One Swiss pilot, his Me-109E riddled from nose to tail, and himself wounded with bullets in his lungs and his legs, managed a crash landing, which he survived. The second 109E shot up the Me-110 that had delivered the damage to his wingman but had to break off combat when Me-110s began firing from all sides. The Swiss pilot dove at full throttle into a deep ravine, hoping the Germans would follow. The latter wanted no part of flying down an unknown gorge and gave up pursuit.

What the Swiss pilot didn't know, but found out soon, was that his aim was better than he'd believed. Minutes after he landed he learned the Me-110 had been crippled by his fire and the twin-engined fighter had crash-landed successfully, the crew being taken prisoner. That, however, was only the first phase of the air battle still building up.

Twelve more Swiss 190Es, scrambled to the scene, hit the Me-110s in a fierce diving attack. The Swiss formation broke up and a wild dogfight over the mountains spread airplanes for miles in every direction. When the melee ended all the Swiss fighters were in the air, but three more Me-110s had gone down, crashing on Swiss soil.

This ended for some time the fighting. The French surrendered and the Germans found little need to continue their provocations of the Swiss. The next month the Swiss found their fighter ranks unexpectedly brought back to full strength. Two Me-109F fighters landed in Switzerland, low on fuel after their pilots became lost. They were immediately taken over by the Swiss, who considered the 109F fighters as excellent replacements for the 109C and 109E airplanes shot down by the Germans. (Two years later the Swiss gained two Me-109G fighters through similar circumstances.)

By 1943 the Swiss had new wrinkles in their problems of airspace violations. American bomber crews sometimes with engines shot out or badly crippled would if possible head for the Swiss border in preference to becoming German prisoners. The planes were often in such bad shape it was imperative they land as quickly as possible, a task assigned to Swiss patrols of four fighters each; two fighters led the crippled bomber toward a field while the other two fighters took up position astern of the bomber. The latter was a safety measure to prevent a bomber pilot from turning for home if he managed to overcome the difficulties with his aircraft. The Swiss felt that once the border had been crossed the aircraft and its crew were wholly under Swiss jurisdiction.

Sometimes, however, this arrangement produced its own crises, as happened on 5th September 1944, when four Swiss Me-109Es escorted a battered Liberator into Dubendorf airdrome. They were only ten miles from the airfield when one of the Me-109Es exploded suddenly in flames. His wingman, the second plane trailing the B-24, was stunned to see an American Mustang sweeping in, wing guns blazing, as he attacked what he obviously believed to be German fighters firing at the B-24. The Mustang made several strikes against the Me-109E, sending it smoking out of the sky until the pilot managed a crash-landing. At that point the P-51D broke off his attacks and headed back for England – with two Messerschmitts to be tacked onto his credited kills!

The Me-109K-14 was the last of the fighter line to see mass production and, in the form of two aircraft, the last of the production line to get into combat. Had the war lasted longer, other Me-109 variants (and sub-variants), as well as offshoot ideas from the basic airplane, would have found their way into the air. The Me-109L grew from the late-model 109G fighters and was to be redesigned around the new Junkers Jumo 213E engine of 1,750 horsepower. To com-

pensate for the larger size of the 213E engineers redesigned the 109 airframe to a greater cross section that would more easily accommodate the new powerplant. The wingspan was increased to improve control at low speeds and to bring to a halt the steady increase in wing-loading which by now was exceeding forty three lbs per sq ft. The maximum speed, without power boost, would have been 474 mph.

When Allied troops overran the Caudron-Renault research complex in France they put a sudden end to the Me-109S project, which was intended to retain high-speed performance but improve low-speed control and handling. The 109S was within three months of completion when the complex was swept within the Allied advance. A research aircraft, the Me-109V24 (which had been used with the Me-309 program), was being rebuilt into the Me-109S configuration. By placing a large scoop beneath the fuselage for ram effect, engineers hoped to duct a flow of pressurized air behind the main spar, and out across the control surfaces and the flaps; the air would issue from narrow slots along the top wing surface. As with the projected Me-109L, engineers were running into the problem of the small Me-109 fuselage, and the S model, as with the L, would have had a larger fuselage section.

Another high-altitude fighter was being developed from the Me-109G-5; this received the designation P.1091/1, and was distinguished from the 109G-5 through a larger tail. Messerschmitt notes indicate that the airplane would be powered with a DB-605A engine – with a DB-603 engine installed to drive the powerful supercharger at heights above 50,000 feet. One 30-mm and two 20-mm cannon were to be fitted.

The P.1091/2 was the same design modified to a larger fuselage and wings of greater span for better handling in the thin air of high altitude. Still a third model was proposed, the P.1019/3, with the fuselage again redesigned, a DB-603 engine with a new supercharger, and contra-rotating four-bladed propellers fitted for better performance at high altitude.

The Me-109Z (*Zwilling*-Twin) has already been noted; this was the project in which two Me-109G fuselages, most of the wings and internal equipment, would be mated into a single large twin-boomed long-range fighter. As an attack or destroyer aircraft the 109Z was to be equipped with five 30-mm cannon and a bomb load of 1,100 pounds. When used primarily as a bomber it would carry two 30-mm cannon and a 4,400-pound bomb load. A final version proposed would have had two Juno 213 engines with a combined total of 3,500 horsepower fitted to the airplane.

The Me-209 has been discussed in detail earlier in these pages. However, there is an entirely separate program – without any relation to the Me-209 that was passed off to the public as the Me-109R. This was known as the Me-209V5 (or, alternatively, Me-209-11), and was based on the Me-109G aircraft. The 209V5 program was intended to produce a fighter that would outfly and outfight the Focke-Wulf FW-190D and the Ta-152, late-model FW-190 versions of outstanding performance. The key to getting the 209V5-series accepted was not to build an entirely new machine, which would have brought about unacceptable delays in tooling for production. From the beginning then, the 209V5 was a mixture of compromises, and yet it carried every new innovation possible to gain the performance that Messerschmitt's design team was trying to attain. Most historians feel the Me-209V5 designation was a sham that would disguise a 'new' fighter-design effort by Messerschmitt. In any event, the final airplane, a modified Me-109F-1 which was rebuilt into the Me-109V31, looked like a bastardization of both the Me-109G and the FW-190. It used a wide, inward-folding main gear; a DB-603 engine as a temporary measure (the DB-628 for high-altitude performance was slated to be installed later); and mounted both cannon and machine guns within the wings. The first flight with the DB-603A engine of 1,750 hp was made on 3rd November 1943 by Fritz Wendel (who set the speed record in the Me-209). Nine days later the new engine, the DB-603G of 1,900 hp, was installed and the airplane flown again.

For the next eight months the airplane was extensively tested in the air. Major changes were made until the modifications list began to obscure the origin of the machine. Even the engines had to be abandoned as a future item; the DB-603G was being snarled in production-line difficulties and Messerschmitt was forced to turn to the Jumo 213E engine. This meant redesigning the airplane (again!) to take the larger engine. The second prototype was known as the Me-209V-6 and, after different propeller tests, was scheduled for production as the Me-209A-2. The 209V-6 first flew in May of 1944 and engineers were enthusiastic about its performance. But by then, with the FW-190D and the Ta-152 in full production, the Me-209A-2 project got the axe – all development was to be stopped in favour of the Focke-Wulf fighters already in service.

The Me-209V5 was fed into the P.1091 project (noted above), which also saw the use of the Me-109V49 and 109V50. Another Me-109G-5 was brought into the program to become the prototype for the Me-109H. This airplane finally was again modified to take the tail of the Me-209V5, along with a larger wing, and was re-designated the Me-109V54. Tests with these fighters began in the late spring of 1943. The second Me-209 prototype, the 209V6, redesignated the Me-109V55, served as the prototype for the Me-109H.

There was still another high-altitude fighter development as part of the Me-209 series; this was to parallel the Me-109H programme. The prototype flew in June 1944, using the DB-603G engine, and plans were being carried out to install the DB-627 at a later date. Initial flight tests were extremely promising, but the advance of Allied armies interrupted the program so many times it was finally dropped.

Still another fighter design, and wholly separate from all those discussed, was the Me-309, a project begun in 1940, and intended to parallel the Me-209 program. The Messerschmitt team apparently had more faith in the Me-209 design and was inclined to treat the 309 as something of a stepchild. Many Me-309 features, including wide-track conventional landing gear, tricycle landing gear, retractable radiators and

The Me-155B-1 was perhaps the oddest of the 109 variants with the 'Zwilling' twin fuselage project, and from this illustration it is possible to see the extent to which the basic 109 design could be adapted

coolers, and cockpit pressurization systems, were tested on a group of 109F models rebuilt into the Me-109V24, 109V31, 109V30 and 109V30A. By the time these were flying the German government's enthusiasm for the project was barely lukewarm, and the original program was scaled down drastically to include only nine experimental machines. Once again the cooling of official ardor resulted from the fear of interfering with pro-

duction, which tooling for a new fighter would have demanded.

In June 1942 the Me-309V1 rolled out of the factory. Even during taxi tests the technical problems were so severe that the aircraft wasn't ready for its flight test until 18th July 1942 – and that was something of a minor disaster when the cooling system failed and the pilot had to land quickly, after only seven minutes in the air. The tricycle undercarriage, with which the Germans had little experience, gave them all kinds of trouble. In its main purpose, to overcome the tendency of swinging during takeoff, the tricycle gear system failed completely. In a desperate attempt to get rid of the problem that seemed to curse Messer-

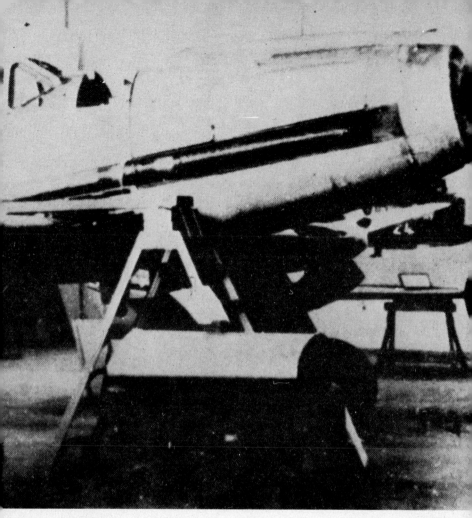

schmitt designs, engineers placed five different tail assemblies on the airplane – all, apparently, unsuccessful.

The initial prototype was wrecked so many times in taking off and landing that it cut back sharply on the planned building of nine machines. So many parts and pieces were rushed from the plant to get the patched-up Me-309V1 back into the air that only four entire airplanes could be built. From beginning to end the 309 was a failure. Finally, with the tremendous promise in the Me-262 jet fighter, the 309 program was concluded, and the airplanes were used in armament, seat ejection, and cockpit pressurization tests for the Me-262.

Few of Messerschmitt's designs became so embroiled in conflict between designers, competitive companies, and the government as did the Me-155. Unlike the 209 or 309 projects (or even the 409, which was to be an enlarged 309) the Me-155 stemmed directly from the Me-109G. In effect it was a belated pickup of the old Me-109T, the carrier-based version of the Me-109E. That project had been abandoned, but in 1942 renewed plans to get the *Graf Zeppelin* carrier onto the high seas as an operational warship brought on the need for a new carrier-based fighter of high performance. But as had happened before, the *Graf Zeppelin*, as well as plans for other carriers, went down the drain and the Me-155, after initial designs had been

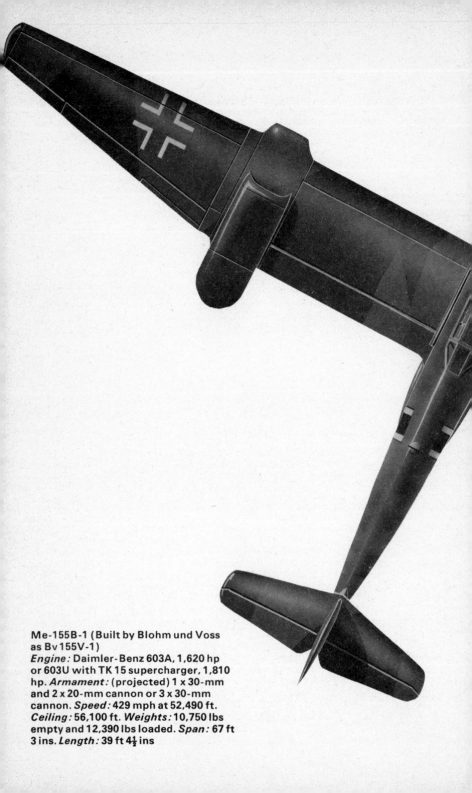

Me-155B-1 (Built by Blohm und Voss as Bv155V-1)
Engine: Daimler-Benz 603A, 1,620 hp or 603U with TK 15 supercharger, 1,810 hp. *Armament:* (projected) 1 x 30-mm and 2 x 20-mm cannon or 3 x 30-mm cannon. *Speed:* 429 mph at 52,490 ft. *Ceiling:* 56,100 ft. *Weights:* 10,750 lbs empty and 12,390 lbs loaded. *Span:* 67 ft 3 ins. *Length:* 39 ft 4½ ins

made up, was abandoned in its original form. As a carrier fighter it was to have the DB-605A of 1,475 hp and the heavy armament of three 20-mm cannon and two 13-mm guns. Despite the heavy carrier equipment – strengthened gear, catapult spool, arrestor hook, etc – its speed was estimated at 403 mph.

The Me-155, stillborn in the design stage, received a new lease on life as the Me-155A – a fighter-bomber version which had all carrier gear removed, the tailwheel modified, guns reduced and fuel increased, and was capable of carrying a 2,200-pound bomb. The Air Ministry, however, turned down the Messerschmitt proposal.

Messerschmitt went back to the drawing board and came up with what the Luftwaffe needed urgently in late 1942 and early 1943 – the design for a high-altitude fighter of outstanding performance. Messerschmitt proposed use of a three 20-mm cannon fighter with the DB-628 engine, then being prepared for its first flight tests. But again the Air Ministry turned Messerschmitt down for its new Me-155B proposal, stating that Messerschmitt was too involved in its own programs, and that they should turn everything on the Me-155B over to Blohm and Voss. Blohm and Voss redesigned the machine drastically, including placing the cooling radiators and gear housings well out on the wings. The BV-155V1, as it was now designated, crashed on a test flight and the second model, the BV-155V2, was still on the ground when the war ended.

Messerschmitt's Me-109TL project, which began in 1943, was a combination of the Me-109, the Me-409, and the Me-155B. Meetings early in 1943 led to this machine, which ended up finally as the Me-109 jet fighter proposal.

The program had its first steps when the Air Ministry asked Messerschmitt if the 2,000 hp DB-603 engine could be used in a re-designed Me-109 fighter, instead of in the Me-309 which had already shown signs of being a great disappointment. If the new 2,000 hp aircraft were successful, would it then be possible to reduce the production of the Me-262 jet? A group of Me-262A-O fighters were already flying and Messerschmitt had

on order 130 Me-262s for the 262A-O and 262A-1 variants.

Messerschmitt looked into the possibility of a jet-powered Me-109 fighter. It didn't take his engineers long to confirm that the 109 design itself wouldn't work out, *but*, they noted, the Me-155B design could well be adapted to jet engines. It had the same wing as the Me-409 design, which was well suited to the jet fighter proposal. The new redesign called for removal of the DB-603 engine. In its place would go a nosewheel (from the Me-309) and auxiliary fuel tanks. Two Jumo 004-B turbojets would be slung beneath the wings in the same fashion as the Me-262, and armament would comprise one 20-mm and two 30-mm cannon. The more they looked at the Me-155B jet proposal the more obvious it became that other changes would be necessary. That meant a larger tail. The landing gear would have to be tricycle, as planned, but that brought the engineers full circle to their first dilemma – the Air Ministry wanted the new jet to utilize as many components of the 109 fighter as was possible. As it turned out the airplane would have to be almost a completely new design and unavoidably would interfere with the 109 production line.

Thus the Me-155B went the way of other Me-109 offshoots – relegated to the *Cancelled* file. But in this case it was a Messerschmitt – the Me-262 – that replaced a Messerschmitt.

Epilogue

By the end of World War II the German aircraft industry had produced a total of 30,573 variants of the basic Me-109 fighter aircraft.

Czechoslovakia and Spain, which continued to produce the Me-109 in foreign variants after the war, brought the grand total to more than 33,000 aircraft – the greatest number of airplanes ever built of one type.

After the defeat of Germany the Czechs continued their production of the Me-109G-14, which was powered with the DB-605 engine. The Avia Works at Cakovice, primary manufacturer, redesignated the Me-109G-14 as the Avia C10. To provide training aircraft, the Me-109G-12 two-seat trainer was continued in production as the Avia C110. After some years, when the supply of DB-605 engines was virtually exhausted, the Avia Works engineers modified the airplanes to take the Jumo 211F, changing the C10 designation to the C210. Among the changes was a shift to a new propeller of Junkers design, with greatly increased blade surface area. This improved performance in some respects, but at the same time inter-fered so severely with normal flying characteristics that the airplane earned a reputation as a vicious and unpredictable machine to handle – and worthy of the name adopted for the C210 by its pilots – *Mezek*, or Mule.

The Czech variants of the Me-109G-14, as the Avia C210, were destined to continue the 109's long record of combat flying begun in the Spanish Civil War. An order for C210s was delivered to Israel where, along with Spitfires obtained elsewhere, it shared honours as the first of the single-seat fighters of the newborn Israeli Air Force. These airplanes later scored tremendous one-sided victories against Egyptian Spitfires which, agreed the pilots flying for the Israelis, 'had no business in the air'. Chalmers H Goodlin, who made the first unpowered tests in the Bell XS-1 rocket-powered research aircraft, flew one of the C210s in Israel, shooting down three Spitfires (among other kills).

Spain, which had been receiving Me-109 fighters since the late thirties, was among the several nations that used the Me-109 in different variants

Hispano HA-1112-M-1-L
Engine: Rolls-Royce Merlin 500-45, 1,400 hp. *Armament:* 2 x 20-mm cannon and 8 x 80-mm rockets. *Speed:* 419 mph at 13,120 ft. *Ceiling:* 33,450 ft. *Range:* 476 miles. *Weights:* 5,855 lbs empty and 7,011 loaded. *Span:* 36 ft 6½ ins. *Length:* 29 ft 10½ ins

as a first-line fighter for many years. Shortly after the Spanish Civil War ended the Spanish Air Force was re-organized, and new designations given to the many types of foreign aircraft then in use. The Me-109B-2 became the Spanish C4, the 109E-1 the C5. New fighters were redesignated as they were received from Germany, fifteen Me-109F-3 models having their desig-nation changed to the Spanish C10. Since the chances of getting any more fighters from other countries during World War II were almost nil, the Spanish arranged to put the Me-109 into production under license. Hispano-Aviacion S.A. launched its

program to build two hundred Spanish versions of the Me-109G-2; Germany agreed to assist the effort by sending to Spain twenty-five disassembled G-2 fighters to familiarize the Spanish technicians in assembling and learning the details of the aircraft. The wings and airframes arrived in due time but the engines were never delivered – and the Spanish 109G-2s were on their way to complete 'internationalization' when the Spanish decided to install into the G-2 fighters the Hispano-Suiza HS 12-Z-89 engine, which was itself a modification of the French Hispano-Suiza 12Y power-plant.

With installation of the 1,300 hp engines, the Spanish had to modify their version of the G-2, since the Spanish engine rotated in a direction opposite that of the Daimler-Benz. For takeoff with the 12-Z-89 engine the pilot used left rather than right rudder to compensate for torque. Tests were made with American pro-

pellers until a shipment of Swiss props could be received. Finally, the first Spanish models of the 109G-2 took to the air early in 1946, and twenty-five aircraft were delivered by January 1947.

Different versions were built, running the designations from HA-1109J-1-L to HA-1190K-1-L, K-2-L and K-3-L. These aircraft, which the Spanish Air Force designated as the C4J, included several models powered with the British Merlin engine. Armament varied from 20-mm cannon to 80-mm rocket missiles. A two-seat trainer was also built, following the basic design of the Me-109G-12.

With the Merlin engine installed the speed of the aircraft was well above 400 mph, although it must be stressed that such speeds were always dependent upon the condition of engines and airframe which, experience showed, could vary greatly from one squadron to another. The airplane, however,

served the Spanish well, and it was continued in production until 1958.

Twenty-three years' production for a fighter airplane – starting before the Spanish Civil War and continuing well past the Korean War–speaks for itself.

Today the Me-109 fighter, in its different variants, is no longer serving its original role. Yet the airplane, fortunately for those who believe in continuing a great machine, will remain in service for a long time to come.

Of course its surroundings have changed. At Rebel Field in Mercedes, Texas, a group of pilots and businessmen devoted to the great airplanes of World War II have for many years supported the Confederate Air Force.

And there the last Me-109 fighters may be seen – in the good company of Lightnings, Mustangs, Warhawks, Thunderbolts, Wildcats and Hellcats, Airacobras, and other great fighter names of aviation history.

Bibliography

Air Force Caidin, Martin, New York:
Holt, Rinehart & Winston, 1957.
Black Thursday Caidin, Martin, New York: E P Dutton & Co. 1960,
Thunderbolt! Caidin, Martin and Johnson, Robert, New York:
Holt, Rinehart & Winston, 1958,
Army Air Forces in World War II W F Craven and
J L Cate, eds. Chicago: University of Chicago Press, 1948-51.
The First and the Last Galland, Adolf,
New York: Rinehart & Winston, 1954,
Famous Fighters of the Second World War Green, William,
New York: Hanover House.
Wing Leader G. E. Johnson, New York: Ballantine Books 1957.
I Flew for the Führer Knoke, Heinz,
New York: Rinehart & Winston, 1954.
The German Air Force Lee, Asher, New York: Harper & Row, 1946.
Strike from the Sky McKee, Alexander,
Boston: Little, Brown & Co., 1961.
The Messerschmitt 109 Nowarra, Heinz, London: Harleyford, 1963.
Messerschmitt ME-109 Nowarra, Heinz, Fallbrook, California: Aero Publishers 1963.
History of the Royal Air Force, 1939-45, Richards, Denis and Saunders, Hilary
St G, London: Her Majesty's Stationery Office, 1961.